To LYNDA,

GW01418765

Thank you for 9 incredible
years ~ Benidorm.

love Alan & Christine
16/12/21

LIVING
UNDER FIVE FLAGS.

MY LIFE & MINISTRY IN
CHALLENGING TIMES.

BOOK ONE.

THE LORD TOOK ME!

LIVING IN SOUTHERN RHODESIA
&

RHODESIA

By

Alan (AB) Robertson

Living Under Five Flags
© 2021 by Alan (AB) Robertson
ISBN 978-1-8384255-1-7
Published by Caracal Books
United Kingdom. https://www.facebook.com/CaracalBooks

The internet addresses, email addresses, and phone numbers in this book are accurate at the time of publication.

FOREWORD

I gladly write a few lines to introduce Alan Robertson's reminiscences and commend them to not only those from Southern Africa or the Rhodesian diaspora but to those in the Lord's Ministry worldwide. The author is a fellow countryman and provides a candid portrait of his life in the unique setting of the more 'British than Britain' Crown Colony of what was Rhodesia in Southern Africa, today Zimbabwe. He has a story worth telling lest it falls into the realm of Almost forgotten -never told. Missionary explorer David Livingstone's discovery of the Victoria Falls on the Dark continent in relatively recent times, namely 1855, saw his appeals for 'Heaven's Command' to bring the Gospel, along with Civilisation, into Central Africa. These recollections reflect our Saviour's call and purposes upon Alan's life as a missionary, statesman and church planter, where we see his character, zeal and dedication.

If Christ were indeed divine, no person of ordinary intelligence would question that he had the power to open the eyes of the blind, the ears of the deaf, and the lips of the dumb. If he had the power to forgive sins and give eternal life, it was a small matter to believe he had the power to heal diseases and restore broken lives. In Alan, we see God's call on his life and the journey with a faith profoundly principled on taking God at his word. His service is truly in a Pioneer environment in a land where the die was cast in all things Colonial and where the Government school and education system was very Anglican.

The reader will embark through a kaleidoscope journey in a pioneer land, later buffeted by the 'Winds of Change,' be it UDI, the rise of Nationalism, war or political upheaval. A land mostly devoid of the British class system's blight and where a Jewish fireman on the railway can receive a knighthood and become the Prime Minister. This book appeals to all, and whether you are Zimbabwean or from the former Rhodesia, here is a trip down memory lane. The canvas is vast and abounds with many scriptural gems. The church leader will find many practical applications learnt the hard way and admire Alan's faithfulness to the Ministry, where its fruits are seen worldwide in his disciples around the world in the diaspora from the land of Five flags.

Ian Jamieson
Warwickshire, England.

INTRODUCTION

THE WORLD SCENE

It is hard to believe that so much has changed during my lifetime! The worst war in history ended in Europe on the 8th of May 1945, just five months after I was born. Sadly, although the war ended in Europe, it was to continue in the Far East until the Japanese surrendered on the 2nd September 1945, and The Second World War was finally over!

Before this terrible war started, it was said that the sun never set upon the British Empire for a short time afterward. The first and second World Wars resulted in the Great British Empire's demise and a major shift of power! Indeed, within a few short years of the war, the British Empire was no more! It had gone the way of all previous Empires before and since; a new superpower, the United States, held the position Britain had previously enjoyed.

Having defeated Hitler and Mussolini in Europe and Japan in the Far East, a new threat arose almost immediately. The Soviet Union took control of Eastern Europe, and what is referred to as the Cold War began. The USSR threat became a nightmare and the danger of a Nuclear War a significant concern!

That was not all, as following Japan's defeat in the Far East, another threat arose! This threat arose from the Chinese Communist Party and their involvement in establishing and supporting other Communist regimes that arose in the Far East. At one time, it seemed that nothing could stop the advance of these Communist-dominated countries, which were a threat to peace-loving democracies worldwide.

When I was growing up in Africa, the threat of Nuclear War seemed very remote, but the threat from Russian and Chinese Communists was very real. All over Africa, wherever there were rebellions or insurrections, it was apparent that the Communists were involved. They may not have originated the uprising, but they were always there to support the rebels with arms and ammunition, etc.

I was born into this world, and it is the backdrop to my story!

SOUTHERN RHODESIA

Around fifty years before the Second World War started, a small country in Africa was occupied by the British during the height of the 'Scramble for Africa.' Although it was small compared to many other countries in Africa, it was still almost twice the United Kingdom's size.

There were two main reasons for this occupation. The first was to stop the other interested parties from occupying the country. These interested parties included the Boers in the Transvaal, the Portuguese in Mozambique and Angola, and the Germans in East and West Africa. The great Imperialist, Cecil John Rhodes, dreamt of building a railway across British territory, from the Cape of Good Hope on the Southernmost tip of Africa to Cairo in Egypt in the far North. It would not help his goal if others took over this country.

However, that was not the only reason for the occupation! The second reason was the belief that the territory possessed enormous amounts of gold! Cecil

John Rhodes believed another 'Rand Gold Field' was as rich as the one discovered in the Transvaal. With that in view, he sought and acquired the British government's permission to establish the British South Africa Company.

He also received a concession from Lobengula, the Matabele King, to establish mines throughout his kingdom. The Matabele ruled the whole of the territory we now call Zimbabwe, but, what many forget, is that the Matabele were also recent immigrants! They entered the country from what is now South Africa less than 50 years before the British. The King's father, Mzilikazi, fled from Shaka, the founder of the Zulu nation. After leaving a path of destruction through South Africa, he crossed the Limpopo and settled in what became known as Matabeleland establishing his capital in Bulawayo.

Having gained permission to enter the country from Lobengula, the Pioneer Column of the British South Africa Company arrived in what later became Salisbury on the 12th September 1890. The story is too involved to tell here; however, the country became a British Colony within a few short years. During the following years, the settlers were given the opportunity of joining up with South Africa, but they rejected the offer during a referendum in 1922 in favour of going alone. As early as 1923, only 33 short years after the Pioneer Column hoisted the Union Jack in Salisbury, Southern Rhodesia became a self-governing British Colony with its own flag.

My story is of a white boy growing up in a country in Africa with large open spaces and a small population. When I went to school, the entire population was around 3,500,000 people, including black and white citizens. Before the changeover to 'black rule' in 1980, the white population never exceeded 300,000. It was a lovely country, and I count myself very blessed to have grown up and lived the greater part of my life in this wonderful land.

A few years ago, Tim King asked me to write the foreword of a book he had written called *In Search of Ophir*, which dealt with the history of the 'Assemblies of God' in Rhodesia/Zimbabwe between 1952-1985. I wrote the foreword as requested and furnished him with information about my ministry up and down Zimbabwe. As a result, he suggested that I write a book dealing with my experiences during those years. Tim's suggestion was all the encouragement that I needed to proceed as I had considered writing a book about my ministry but not seriously.

However, when I considered how to begin, I realised that I could not write my story without placing it in the context of those times and of who I am as a person. As a result, I have referred to place names as they were when I grew up and have only used their new names as and when they were changed. In *Book One*, I have spent a lot of time dealing with my early years, followed by how the Lord called me into the ministry. It is only after that, in *Book Two*, that I have been able to consider my life as a Minister of the Gospel in the country now called Zimbabwe.

I Have written this book almost exclusively from my memories of these events. On occasion, I have had to do some investigation to check the historical accuracy of what I have written, but the rest is purely as I remember those days.

In this first book, I want to give thanks to God for

all my family, friends and workmates who helped make me what I am today. Then I want to thank God for those ministers and individual Christians who opened my eyes to the truth of the Gospel. I trust that your efforts have proved to be 'seed' sown on good ground. Finally, I want to thank the Lord for being so patient with me. Praise God that He never gave up on me. "Thank You, Jesus!"

My life has not always been easy, but it has without a doubt been interesting. I trust that you, the reader, will be blessed as we travel down this road together.

Alan (AB) Robertson

THE EARLY YEARS

Chapter 1.

BULAWAYO

BULAWAYO CITY HALL.

A BRIEF FAMILY HISTORY

I was born on the 9th December 1944, at the Lady Rodwell Nursing Home in Bulawayo, Southern Rhodesia, the last of four children born to Alwyn and Jessie Robertson. All four of us were born in December, three years apart. All of us except my eldest brother were born in Bulawayo. He was born in Twickenham in England. After I was born, there were another three birthdays in December. My brother Osmond turned six on the 15th December, my sister Avril, three years old, on the 20th December, and finally, my brother Christopher who turned nine on the 28th December 1944.

My grandfather, Henry John (Harry) Robertson, was born on the 21st March 1864 in Broxbourne, Hertfordshire, England, while my grandmother Emilie Fredricka Robertson (Carlsson) was born in the Cape of Good Hope, in South Africa. The Carlsson's originally came from Sweden, probably emigrating to South Africa around the same time as the 1820 British settlers. My father, Alwyn Broadhurst Robertson, was born in Jeppes Town, Johannesburg, in South Africa, on the 1st of April 1906. He was the second eldest of a family of five boys and one girl.

My grandfather, Harry Robertson, ran away from school in England when he was 14 years old and found work on a 'windjammer' bound for India. Sometime later, he made his way to the goldfields of Kalgoorlie and Coolgardie in Australia. Then at the age of 35, he travelled to South Africa with the Gray Scouts during the Boer War of 1899-1902. At the end of the war, he moved up to Rhodesia, where he met and married Emilie Carlsson, who lived on the farm 'Insindene' in Insiza not far from Bulawayo.

**TWO GRAYS SCOUTS IN THE BOER WAR.
HARRY ROBERTSON ON THE LEFT.**

As she was unwilling to move with him back to Australia, he remained in Rhodesia, working in various places around the country wherever he could. However, after two heart attacks, they moved down to South Africa, believing that living at a lower altitude would be better for his health. Sadly he died in 1919 at the age of 55 and was buried in Namaqualand.

He left a wife with a young family of five sons and one daughter to support. I cannot imagine how the family survived without my grandmother moving back to the farm at Insiza in 1919. Her brother Johan Carlsson and his wife, Ellee, and her sister, Aggy, made room for them to live at 'Insindene' on the farm. At the time of Harry's death, only his eldest son, Cyril, had been to school, meaning none of the rest of the family had had any education. However, living at 'Insindene,' they all became handy on the farm. I never had the privilege of meeting my grandmother Emilie as she died just before I was born in May 1943.

Sometime later, four of the boys, which must have included my father, although he never mentioned it as far as I remember, were sent to 'Daiseyfield', an orphanage run by the Dutch Reformed Church. As it was an entirely Afrikaans institution and they were the only English-speaking boys in the place, it appears that life was pure hell for the four young Robertson's, which resulted in them running away and hiding out amongst the hundreds of Kopjies in the Matopos hills. One of my uncles told me that it took the Police and Army's combined efforts to locate them. Thankfully, they were only required to spend one term at 'Daiseyfield', but their experiences in this church-run institution affected them all of their lives, causing them to harden their hearts to the Gospel message.

My father's eldest brother, Cyril, and his youngest brother, Noel, with some difficulty, managed to complete their education, enabling them to rise to the top of their chosen careers. Uncle Cyril became the Regional Superintendent of the Railways based in Salisbury before retiring. He was so well respected that when I started work, I learned that the Eastern Region of the Rhodesia Railways was affectionately known as 'Robbie's Railways.' Uncle Noel joined the 'Native Department' and later became a Native Commissioner and, before retiring, rose to the position of Under Secretary to the Ministry of Internal Affairs. Sadly, my father and his other brothers were not so fortunate.

My father and three of his brothers, Cyril, Leslie, and Ivor, all found employment with Rhodesia

Railways, which had its headquarters in Bulawayo, and was a significant employer. My dad ended up in the workshops where he stayed all his working life and his brothers Leslie and Ivor found employment with the running staff.

Despite holding down a full-time job, my father also worked as a Barman at the weekends to support his growing family. I remember him working at several different establishments in Bulawayo, including 'The Railway Recreation Club,' the 'Royal British Legion,' and 'Tattersalls,' which my brother Chris described as a 'drinking and gambling place.' However, when not working, he enjoyed playing rugby at 'Bulawayo Athletic Club' (BAC), and I have a photo of him as the Captain of the 1st team around 1935. It was a pretty rough game in those days as there was not much grass on the rugby fields in Bulawayo.

BAC 1ST TEAM RUGBY. ALWYN ROBERTSON (CAPTAIN) BEHIND HIM TO THE RIGHT IS HIS BROTHER IVOR ROBERTSON

My brother Christopher reminded me that dad also had a small herd of around 20 cattle kept at 'Heathfield,' my Uncle Herbert Carlsson's farm. According to my brother, this was my dad's 'bank account' as he would sell one of the herd if there were a significant need in the family.

On my mother's side of the family, my grandfather, Osmond Boyes, married Dorothy Kingston, and they were blessed with five girls and one boy. My mother, the eldest child, Jessica Gwendolyn Boyes, was born on the 15th of April 1906 in Twickenham, England.

Of their six children, my mother, the eldest, left England to travel to South Africa and finally settled in Southern Rhodesia. Her brother, Stuart, went to live in New Zealand before moving to Canada, where another one of my mother's sisters and her family also went to live. The remaining three daughters remained in England. Sadly, one of my mother's sisters died relatively young, leaving three young children; another sister who had failed to have children adopted one of them. My mother's youngest sister, Diana, never married. She later gave up her job to stay at home and care for her elderly parents.

After graduating from the Royal College of Music in London, my mother left England and travelled to South Africa. She arrived in South Africa in the early 1930s where she worked briefly at 'Firgrove', a country tea room located between Cape Town and 'The Strand.' She then joined a female band that travelled up to Southern Rhodesia. There she and her fellow musicians performed in the 'Lyons Tea Rooms' in Bulawayo, where I believe she must have met my father. After getting married and settling in Bulawayo, she became a founder member of the Bulawayo Municipal Orchestra. She also assisted with the family finances by teaching Piano and Violin.

Whenever the extended family got together, my mother, called 'Chick' by all my father's relatives, would be asked to play either her violin or the piano. Being an accomplished musician who loved to play, she was happy to oblige and entertain all present. Although she trained in classical music, she could turn her hand to all sorts of music and gladly played traditional Scottish, Irish, English, and Afrikaans songs to our great enjoyment. On other occasions, others would ask her to accompany them with the piano as they sang to us. My Uncle Charles McCormack would usually sing, and one of his favourites was *O Sole Mio*. He had a great voice, and I still believe that few can sing that song as well as he did.

Aunt Dot Carlsson, was another one in the family asked to sing. I can almost hear her now as she sang *Bless This House* accompanied by my mother on the piano. However, although they were the leading performers, there were others as well. On one occasion, when I was around six years old, I entertained the gathering by singing *There's a Hole in My Bucket*. I do not remember who sang the part of Lisa, but it was possibly my sister. Our rendering of this famous song was nowhere near as good as that of my Uncle Charles or my Aunt Dot, but as a six-year-old and a nine-year-old, our singing was very well received!

Before leaving the subject of my mother's musical ability, I would like to mention that she did her best to pass on her musical talents to her family as any mother would, I am sure. My eldest brother at one stage played the Piano Accordion in 'Marsicano's Accordion Band.' (More about the Marsicano School of Music later.) My sister, Avril, became a very accomplished pianist. She practiced at 6.00 am every morning before going to school, whilst I may add, I was still trying to sleep. Although my mother did her best, my brother Osmond did not seem to want to play the piano. However, shortly after leaving school, when working for the Native Department, he did become 'The Rock and Roll King of Beit Bridge,' but whether that counts for 'musical ability,' I do not know?

On one occasion, we all chipped in to buy my mother a birthday present. I am not sure whose bright idea it was, but we bought her an LP (for those born later, a Long-Playing Record) entitled 'Elvis's Greatest Hits.' My mother was a great sport and received it graciously, but I think her present had actually been bought so that we could all listen to the music that was top of the Pops at that time!

I fell in love with the Violin, and even today, it can bring tears to my eyes when it is played. When I heard my mother playing at family gatherings, I was deeply moved by the beautiful music. I learned the piano, swapped to the Violin, and sadly finally gave it all up when I was a teenager. However, that was not the end of my musical career, but I will tell that later in my story!

OUR BULAWAYO HOME

THE ROBERTSON FAMILY
Jessie, Alan and Alwyn, Osmond Avril and Christopher.

By the time I was born, our family lived five miles out of town on a one-acre plot of land at number 11 Orange Grove. A few years before I was born, my father won first prize in a raffle, possibly the first and only time he ever 'won' anything. The first prize was a brand-new Motor Car! However, what my dad needed more than anything was a plot of land where he could build a home for his growing family, so he swapped the car for half the land owned by a friend, Mr. Branfield, who also worked on the Railways, and that was how we came to be living at 11 Orange Grove.

As we did not have municipal water laid on in those days, it was a blessing that there was a well situated in the middle of the original property. The well was positioned on the two new properties' border and provided more than adequate water for both households' needs. Although drought is a recurring problem in Bulawayo, the well only ever ran dry during one terrible drought as far as I can remember. The excellent water supply enabled my father to grow vegetables and flowers, some of which he could sell.

As the area where we lived was sparsely populated, the dirt roads around our home were not very well maintained, so when the rains came, the mud became axle-deep. Cars would get stuck in the mud regularly, providing a great deal of excitement as it usually happened just up the road from where we lived. The roads were only graded once or twice a year and, as a result, were very rough to drive on. They had deep ruts made during the rainy season.

While we are talking about rain, we had a local river called the Umgusa, which was just a dry river bed for most of the year. I can remember carrying a 'billycan' to the Marriot's farm to buy milk from their dairy and having to cross the Umgusa river at a drift. After a heavy storm, when the rains came, it could become a raging torrent in a matter of minutes, making the drift uncrossable as the floodwaters covered the road for some distance from the river itself.

Our neighbours, the Branfield's, who lived behind us, had three children. The eldest was Ernest, who represented Southern Rhodesia in cycling, as did his dad. He was selected to represent the country at the Commonwealth Games. Their eldest daughter Patricia was crowned Miss Southern Rhodesia, and then there was the youngest daughter Bridget whom I will mention later. Other neighbours, who lived in the area, included the Knoesen's whose daughter Margaret became a bit of a celebrity when she was selected to dance for the Sadler Wells Ballet Company and left our humble neighbourhood for England. Finally, there was Pete van Staden who boxed for Southern Rhodesia and represented the country at the Commonwealth Games. Although we were living on the 'wrong side' of Bulawayo, the poorer side, we had some neighbours who went on to achieve great things, which was no mean feat for people who lived on the 'wrong side' of town!

Bridget, the Branfield's youngest daughter, trained as a nurse, and later took up a mine hospital position in Northern Rhodesia. She was tragically killed by a brick, smashing through her car window, during a mineworker's riot. As a child, I overheard the conversation that my parents and others had at the time. They were saddened and upset that the people she went to assist in Northern Rhodesia, at some sacrifice to herself, had killed her when she was caught up in a riot that had nothing to do with her. Sadly, as we well know, this story has been repeated many, many times, all over the world.

My Uncle Charles of *O Sole Mio* fame was a professional builder, and he assisted my father in building our family home, or it may well have been the other way around. Our house was a very modest building with several notable features. The most notable was the large veranda that covered the entire front of the house. The rondavel, a large circular building, known as 'The Hut,' sat at the far end of the veranda. 'The Hut' was home to a lovely piano where my mother taught, and my sister practiced the piano. We also used it as our sitting room when not otherwise engaged. Behind 'The Hut,' we had a huge water tank that collected rainwater when it rained and was a real asset during the long dry season.

Once the house was built, Uncle Charles and his wife Gladys, and their two sons, Peter and Michael, stayed with us while he constructed their home on the other side of town. A building behind the water tank, built as a garage, was converted into an outside bedroom. With so many people in the home, it wasn't easy to provide somewhere for everyone to sleep, and so my two brothers and our two cousins all slept in the same double bed, two at one end and two at the other.

During the War and for some years after, The Royal Air-force had a Training base at Heany, approximately 15 miles outside Bulawayo on the Salisbury road. As accommodation was not easy to find in Bulawayo, my mother opened our home to RAF personnel, their wives and their families after Uncle Charles and his family left. As a result, our house was always pretty crowded.

On the great veranda that I have already mentioned, we had a full-size Table Tennis table that provided a great deal of enjoyment to the whole family, provided it was not a windy or rainy day. We had great fun playing singles, doubles, and a game called 'Donkey.' 'Donkey' was played when a group of us would race around the table after hitting the ball in turn. When you failed to return the ball, you received a 'D' followed by an 'O' and so on until you were 'Donkey' and had to leave the game. Eventually, the remaining two players would have to hit the ball and turn around before the ball returned and, hopefully, return the ball successfully. It was a fun game which we all enjoyed playing. However, being the youngest, you can guess who was 'Donkey' first on most occasions.

Not only did my age affect me playing 'Donkey,' but it also was a disadvantage playing singles. On one memorable occasion, unsurprisingly, my eldest brother Chris, who was nine years older than me, beat me at a game of 'Ping Pong,' but he was holding the bat in his mouth!! I did improve, but I have never won against my brother Christopher at table tennis as far as I know.

When I was a bit older, I used to play regularly with my neighbour, Dennis Pedder. He would generally beat me; however, when he suggested that we had a 'competition,' things usually changed, and I would typically win. It is nice to relate that I did improve.

The veranda was also an ideal spot for a dartboard, which also provided a lot of fun. Our home was a great place to grow up. My childhood was wonderful, and I enjoyed life to the full. One of the things that made life great was how my brother Christopher could make us laugh. On one occasion, I remember sitting at the table after a meal when I could not stop laughing. I laughed so much that I fell off my chair, holding my stomach, which was aching so much. Being the eldest, he did push his luck a bit, like the day he arrived home late after we had all eaten. He was sitting at the table having his meal, and I was outside on the veranda when he called me in, and asked, "Alan, could you please pass the salt?"

What a cheek, calling me into the house from outside to pass him the salt!! Despite the cheek of it, I suppose I gave him the salt before continuing with the vital work that I was engaged in outside. He was usually able to get away with anything as we all enjoyed his marvelous sense of humour!

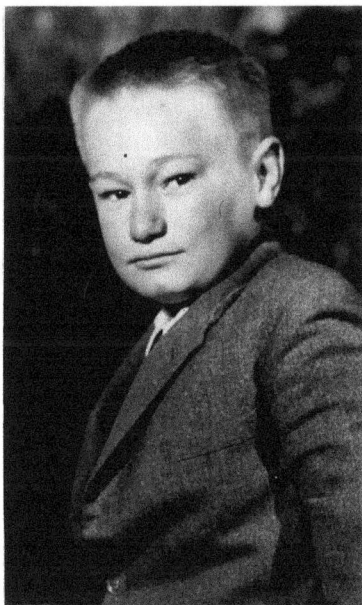

ALAN AT 11 YEARS OLD.

My brother Chris's first job was at Deloitte, Plender, Griffiths, Annan & Co as an articled clerk. He was earning the grand sum of £15.00 a month out of which he was required to pay my mother £5.00 a month for board and lodging, which was only right. He also paid £5.00 a month for his piano accordion lessons, leaving him the grand total of £5.00.

One day when we were at the table eating, my mother produced some lovely strawberries from the garden, and my brother asked if he could have some cream, and when told that there was no cream, he cheekily said, "What do I pay £5.00 a month for?"

He was, of course, joking as my mother always

made sure that we ate well.

We were not well off, and sometimes my clothes were not as good as I would have liked. For example, once, my mother gave me a pair of shorts that were far, far, too big for me. When I complained, she said that I would grow into them. Well, she may have been correct if I still had them; I may have grown into them by now. Despite my objections, I wore my baggy pants, I had no choice, but I never grew into them!

Being the youngest can be tough, and, believe it or not, there were occasions when I gave my older brothers a bit of cheek. Being so much younger than the two of them, they were not impressed with their cheeky young brother, and as a result, on more than one occasion, I had to run for my life. However, despite the occasional problem, I was very fond of my big brothers.

One day, when Osmond had some cash, he went to the shops and bought half a loaf of freshly baked bread. Who could forget the bread from 'Downies Bakery?' The bread from 'Lobels Bakery' was also good, but 'Downies' was, without doubt, the best. My brother, whose hands were not all that clean, took the centre out of the bread and then plastered the inside crust with butter and jam. He then proceeded to eat it in front of us. Can you imagine that? Just thinking about it even now makes my mouth water. As we looked somewhat peckish, he offered my sister and me the bread that he had abandoned! The bread that he had taken out with his dirty hands. I am not sure whether we accepted or not, but most likely we did, as it looked good, particularly the crust that he was eating all by himself!

I have not said much about my sister, Avril. She was always there for me, and I do not doubt that she loved her little brother. She expressed her love when I was very young and ended up in the hospital with Whooping Cough. It was touch and go whether I would make it or not, and because my sister loved me so much, she gave me her favourite rag doll, something that was very dear to her heart. Praise God, I recovered and was soon out of the hospital; however, I have a feeling that when I recovered, she asked for the return of her precious doll.

Despite never having many toys to play with, just a few 'dinks' and a few marbles, we had a great childhood living at 11 Orange Grove. I had an old bike that had belonged to my older brother, then my other brother, then my sister, and finally to me. It had no mudguards, bell, or brakes when it reached me, but it was great. I used to ride all over the place with it, particularly along the bush tracks near our home. It was easy to bring the bike to a stop; all you had to do was put your shoe on the back tyre when you wanted to stop, making sure that you put your shoe on the tyre and not in the spokes! I had great fun with my bike!

Those carefree days nearly came to an abrupt end one hot Summer's day. A friend, Nigel Smith, who lived just down the road, asked me to go around for a swim in his parent's swimming pool, possibly the only swimming pool for miles around in those days. We did not have one at our local school. When I got there, Nigel was not alone as a lady, and her child was also present. However, shortly after I arrived, she and her youngster got out of the pool and left Nigel and me on our own.

I should not have been there without adult supervision as I had not learned to swim. However, I was cautious to have a tube around my waist when I was in the water. I knew that Nigel could swim, and so I was surprised when he started to behave a little strangely. After seeing him go up and down a few times, I realised that something was wrong and leapt into the water with the tube around my waist. He grabbed hold of me, and we somehow managed to make it to the side. Years later, I met him while doing my National Service in the Army, and he took time out to come and thank me again for saving his life that day. Sad to say, that was the first and last time that I went swimming in Nigel's swimming pool. Anyhow, it was not long after that episode that I finally learned to swim!

Before I talk about my school days, I must mention Dennis Pedder again, who became a great friend. His family purchased the house behind ours when the Branfields sold up and moved. He had two sisters, Norma and Sylvia, and a baby brother whose name I have forgotten.

Some years before, when my Father was trying to establish a garden, he discovered that our property's ground was extremely rocky. Instead of giving up, he asked our gardener to use a sieve to remove the stones from the soil. The rocks needed depositing somewhere convenient and out of the way. He found a solution and deposited them along our border fence, and over time the stones became much like a wall between the two properties. Once the rocks were removed and the soil enriched with compost, my Father could grow lovely vegetables and flowers. After providing for our own needs, our gardener sold the rest of the flowers and vegetables to passing motorists on the main road into the city, which was some distance away.

At that time, I loved to listen to the *Tarzan* stories

that Radio Rhodesia used to broadcast, so, when I wanted to contact my friend Dennis, I would go and stand on the pile of stones at the fence, beat my chest and let out a *Tarzan* cry. If he were home, Dennis would appear and call me over as soon as he heard me.

One day, having not seen him for a while and having, first of all, let out my *Tarzan* cry to ascertain that he was at home, I went around to visit. I ended up talking non-stop while he listened patiently. Finally, Dennis interrupted me and pointed out his dad's new tape recorder, which had been recording the whole time. It had recorded all that I said, and after rewinding the tape, he played it back to me. It was amusing hearing myself on tape for the first time, but it made me feel more than a little foolish, listening to myself talking non-stop. It is sobering to realise that what you said could be recorded on tape, without your knowledge even in those days.

On one occasion, Dennis arrived at our house (without doing a Tarzan call, I might add) while I was practising the piano. My mother made sure that I practised for at least half an hour every day whether I wanted to or not. I can hear her even now calling out 'C' or 'D' when I hit the wrong note for the umpteenth time. However, it is sad to say that I was not interested and would often have my knees up on the piano, hoping that the half-hour practice would soon be over. I was amazed at how interested Dennis was and even showed him his first notes on the piano. He later became a fine musician and served with a military band in the UK for some years. He then returned to Rhodesia, where he opened a music school.

Sadly, there is one more story that I need to relate

about my good friend Dennis. One day he arrived at our house to show me his 'new' BSA Bantam Motor Cycle, which I believe his Father had bought for him. Even though it was only a single-seater, he offered to take me for a ride. It had a carrier on the back for luggage not a passenger. Nevertheless, I piled on the back, and we went for a ride. As he was such a good friend, after we had gone some miles, he asked if I wanted to have a go. I took the controls, and we headed out of town towards the newly opened Bulawayo Airport, which was a few miles further on.

Loose gravel covered the tarmac at the turn-off to the Airport. As I began to turn, I realised that I was going too fast, and if I continued, we would skid on the gravel and have an accident. By then, it was too late to correct, and before I knew it, we ended up in the ditch.

When Dennis, who was on the back, realised what was about to happen, he decided that it was safer to hop off rather than stay on the bike. Sadly, he took a nose dive onto the tarmac and loose gravel, resulting in him being badly grazed all over his body. When I left the road, I went straight into a ditch and was thrown forward, catching the inside of my leg just above the knee on the broken handlebars, which created a large wound, the scars of which I still bear today. Having got to my feet, I was horrified to see what had happened to Dennis. Blood was dripping everywhere from the abrasions on his body. On the other hand, he was horrified to see the gaping wound on my leg, which I had not noticed until then.

Shortly after it happened, someone must have stopped and given us a ride to the hospital, where they attended to Dennis and stitched me up. His father arrived and gave us a ride home. I have no idea whether the police were notified or any other details. The motor cycle was repaired, but it was never quite the same, and it is possible our friendship was never quite the same from then on either. However, our lives were already beginning to take different routes, and not long afterwards we lost contact. I never rode that motorcycle again. However, I eventually learned to ride a motorcycle years later and never had another accident by God's grace.

To return to my 'musical career' my mother was my first teacher, and was determined to give me every opportunity to learn, even though I was not all that teachable. My mother then arranged for me to have lessons with Mrs. Roberts at the music school where they taught. On one occasion, when travelling into town for my lesson, I missed the bus, and as the next bus was too late to get me to my lesson on time, I decided to walk and hopefully get a lift. Well, I did get a lift, part of the way, when a kindly African man gave me a ride on his bicycle. I finally arrived a good hour after my lesson should have ended! Mr. Marsicano, the owner of the Music School, was very sympathetic and always used to call me Maestro, a title that I definitely did not deserve.

Before we proceed, I am pretty sure that Mr. Marsicano was Jewish and one of several Jewish people who entered the country in the 1930s and '40s. In the 1930s, several Jewish immigrants arrived in the country from the Island of Rhodes, and later, German Jews were fleeing the Nazis, who came in the 1940s. The Jewish immigrants to our country contributed much to the development of the nation. It is only while writing this book that I realised that Alfred Beit was Jewish. His name will keep cropping up in my story; for example, the bridge across the Limpopo River at the border between South Africa and Southern Rhodesia is Beit Bridge. At my senior school, the school hall was named Beit Hall, both named after this man. Getting back to Mr. Marsicano, I must say that he was a real blessing to our entire family.

MARSICANO SCHOOL OF MUSIC
AVRIL (STANDING) SIXTH FROM THE LEFT
JESSIE ROBERTSON (AT THE BACK) THIRD FROM THE LEFT, JUST TO THE LEFT OF THE CURTAIN, MR MARSICANO (AT THE BACK) SIXTH FROM THE LEFT.

Down the road from where we lived, there was a reservoir on the Hendricksens' property. One night, it would appear that one of our dogs called Brutus had wandered down the road (we had no fence and no gate), and he must have decided to get a drink from the reservoir. That night, however, the reservoir was not full, and we presume that he must have fallen in trying to get a drink. Because the water was so low, he could not get out, and as a result, he drowned and was found dead in the water the next morning. It broke my heart when we had to bury our lovely, gentle dog.

My brother Christopher has told me that the reservoir was built to supply water to irrigate a reasonably large market garden that Mr. Hendricksen had established. They had a son, Ron, and a daughter, Synava, who were great friends of our family. My brother Osmond and Ron produced some well-illustrated comics. Ron went on to be a successful architect, but my brother Osmond never developed his talent in that area, as far as I know.

The Hendricksens had a pet baboon that used to escape and cause much fear in our household. One day disaster nearly struck when their son, Ron, dressed up like a baboon and came around to our house to frighten the family. My dad was home at the time, and when he realised that the baboon was on the loose again, he went and got his .22 rifle and was planning to shoot the beast if it came any closer. I am not sure who spotted that it was Ron, but we were all very grateful that my dad did not shoot the Baboon that day, as that would have been an absolute disaster. There is no doubt that our neighbour, Ron, had a close shave that day!

SOME INTERESTING CHARACTERS IN BULAWAYO

We had many family members living in the Bulawayo area in those days, and the following stories relate some of the interesting characters that were part of my family circle as I remember them. All of the characters were products of their time, and I loved them; they were a real blessing to my family and me.

Herbert Carlsson was my dad's mother's brother, who owned a farm called 'Heathfield' near Filabusi, some miles from Bulawayo. For some years, my father had a small herd of cattle on the farm and would have loved to go into farming. However, somewhere along the line, Uncle Herbert needed extra funds (what farmer does not, at times, need extra money), and on this occasion, his solution was to sell half of the farm. Selling the farm proved relatively straightforward; however, the purchaser wanted the half on which the house stood. No doubt there were many conversations about what to do. Finally, a deal was struck, and Aunt Grace moved into Bulawayo to stay with her daughter and family until Uncle Herbert finished building a new farmhouse.

As a temporary measure, my uncle built a large brick and cement rondavel on a granite outcrop, much like 'The Hut' at our home in Bulawayo. The longterm plan was to build a new house on the farm so that Aunt Grace could move back home. Twice a month, he would come into town to do business and see his wife and family. During the two or three days that he spent in town, he would drink far too much and then return to the farm to sober up, where he never drank at all. Sadly, the new house was still not built when I visited him at his rondavel many years later.

His brother Johan Carlsson had a farm called 'Insindene' in Insiza on the other side of Bulawayo. As mentioned previously, Johan, his wife, Ellee, and her sister, Aggy, lived at 'Insendene.' They provided a home for my grandmother Emilie Robertson after my grandfather died. I can remember visiting several times when my mother would end the evening with some fine music. Anyhow, the story that I heard was that Johan would also go into Bulawayo once a month, where he too would drink too much and drive home that same night. On his way home, I understand that he never stopped to open the farm gates but used to go straight through them. Fortunately, these were gates made from wire and a few poles cut from nearby trees, so they would not do serious damage!

Another brother was my Uncle Kenneth Carlsson. He, together with his wife, Aunt Dot (of *Bless this House* fame), ran an auctioneer's business in Shabane, the primary asbestos mine in Southern Rhodesia, which was a significant world producer of asbestos. We, on occasions, visited them during the school holidays after my father died. They had a large male turkey running wild in the yard, and it was frightening trying to get past when we were in the garden.

On one occasion, there was a 'tandem' bicycle for sale in the auctioneers, and my cousin, Miles Authors, who my uncle and aunt later adopted, suggested that we go for a ride. All the same, this was not a standard two-seater 'tandem'; it was a three-seater, which I believe is called a 'triples.' It was quite an experience riding this bike. I do not know how Miles managed to keep it going with two of us on the back. Not only have I never ridden a 'tandem' with three seats again, but I do not think that I have ever seen another one.

My mother always liked playing tricks on people, and she had purchased a lot of 'tricks' over the years at joke shops! Once, when we were visiting Shabane, she decided to play a trick on Uncle Ken by substituting a plastic egg for his fried egg at breakfast. Before he realised that it was not a real egg, he had cut right through the plastic egg, complaining loudly that the eggs were very hard that morning. He did not appreciate the joke, and my mum could not use the artificial egg again.

My Uncle Charles McCormack was married to my mother's cousin, Gladys, and he was also an interesting character. For example, he would never go to a party without taking along a crate of beer, just in case they ran out. As I have already mentioned, he loved to sing *O Sole Mio*, but I am not sure that a pub with no beer was high on his list of favourite songs.

On one occasion, when we visited Bulawayo, from South Africa, and stayed with him, I asked if I could travel home with him one evening. Sadly, he had had a fair amount to drink, and we ended up in the middle of a roundabout before we finally found our way home. He should not have been driving, and I ought not to have been travelling with him; however, he was a real blessing to the whole family.

The house that he had built in Bulawayo was a lovely property, situated in a much better neighbourhood than the one in which I had grown up. He had provided a place for his two sons in the loft to build an extensive 'Meccano' railway. It was the biggest that I have ever seen and must have cost a bomb. For those unfamiliar with 'Meccano,' it is made of metal and was around long before 'Lego' was invented, and is a little more complicated to put together.

Although there were many more characters in Bulawayo in those early days of my life, there is only one more that I want to mention. The Besters owned a gold mine outside Bulawayo and only operated the mine when they needed some extra cash. They lived very simply, right next door to us, in an old house that I remember as very dark.

SIX MONTHS IN ENGLAND

In 1951, my mother went 'home' to England to see her family. My sister, Avril, and I went with her. The journey from Bulawayo to Cape Town by train, to catch the 'Carnarvon Castle,' our 'Union-Castle' liner, was very exciting. One memory stands out. We arrived at Palapye or Mahalapye Station in Bechuanaland, to the colourful sight of a hoard of vendors descending on the train to sell their wares. When we pulled away, I was the proud possessor of a carved wooden animal.

Sadly, my sister and I were confined to our cabin for almost the entire journey after the ship's doctor diagnosed, we had measles. The trip back from Britain on another 'Union Castle' ship was much more exciting. However, as we passed through the Bay of Biscay, we were banned from going on deck because there was a violent storm. It was such a powerful storm that the First Officer of a nearby ship was swept overboard. They told us that at one point, a wave went as high as the 'crow's nest,' and the whole ship was under water for a moment. The day after we docked in Cape Town, there were pictures of our battered ship on the front page of 'The Cape Times.'

My wife, Mally, and I were privileged to enjoy two wonderful cruises on the Mediterranean many years later. On two of the four trips, we also encountered very violent storms across the Bay of Biscay as we travelled to and from the UK. On our first cruise, we discovered that we were among a minority on board on their first cruise. Most people we met had been on several cruises, and some had been on many, many, cruises.

On our second cruise, when we were going through the second storm, we met up with a couple we knew from the first cruise. The only storms they experienced on the Bay of Biscay during the many cruises they had taken were the two occasions when I was on board. As a result, they told me that they were seriously thinking of arranging to have me thrown overboard! They had concluded that I must be a Jonah and thought it might help if they threw me overboard! Well, as you can see, I did not suffer the indignity of being thrown overboard and praise God; I survived to tell the tale.

It was an experience living in England and staying with my grandparents. They lived at 30 Orford Gardens, Twickenham, and their nearest station was Strawberry Hill.

My grandparents were a real blessing; however, if I listen carefully, I think that I can still hear my grandfather shouting, "Shut That Door!"

Sadly, this happened almost every day when I failed to shut the lounge door where he was sitting and reading next to the fire. It was unnecessary to keep the doors shut in Bulawayo, as the climate was much warmer, so I just kept forgetting.

While we were in England, I enjoyed meeting my cousins, Christopher Chadder, and Michael and Jennifer Fowler. They discovered that I could not tell the time, and I remember them being rather shocked that a boy of six or maybe seven (I turned seven while in England) could not tell the time! Nevertheless, despite them thinking that I was a little ignorant, there was one thing that happened while I was attending the local school that they never forgot.

Yes, believe it or not, I did not have six months holiday while we were in England. I attended the local school. I was surprised that they did not have a sports field but only a 'yard' to play in during break time. In Bulawayo, Kingsdale, the school I attended was relatively small, nothing to write home about, but even we had a playing field! Not a great playing field as it had hardly any grass, but it was still a playing field! It was also a bit of a shock to discover that school did not end at 1.00 pm but finished much later. Nevertheless, at breaktime one day, a little English boy threw a brick at me, resulting in me immediately sorting him out in much the same way that I would have done back home in Bulawayo.

Although I know that you may find this hard to believe, guess what? I got into trouble, and my breaktime came to an abrupt end! I was detained and had to stay inside the classroom for the remainder of the break. As you can imagine, I was not happy. It appeared that you could throw a brick at someone and get away with it, but if you retaliated, you were punished! Not only did I get into trouble at school, but they informed my mother of my 'bad' behaviour. My relatives, including my grandparents, and the neighbours, found out about my behaviour that day, which they never forgot. When I met them many years later, they reminded me of my 'misdeeds' at the local school!

Six months seemed to be a very long time to be away from home, but it was soon over, and we were back in Cape Town, where the rest of the family met us. We returned to Bulawayo by train because my Father was a railwayman and was entitled to free or much-reduced fares. Sadly, having been away from my school for six months, my education had suffered; I may have learned how to tell the time, but I needed extra lessons to catch up with my classmates.

KINGSDALE JUNIOR SCHOOL

As children, we all went to Kingsdale School, a very small Junior School not far from where we lived. Just in case you may have thought that the playground incident in England was a one-off, I sadly confess that I used to get into fights regularly, one of which I remember well. At school one morning, I happened to overhear two older boys telling one of the younger boys that they would beat him up after school. As I objected to bullying (remember that), I told them that it would only be over my dead body. It was only by the grace of God that I survived that day.

One of the boys was my long-term friend Francie De Bryn, and the other was one of his other friends, but not a friend of mine. After school, I instructed the younger boy to get on home while I dealt with the older boys. Once we had left the school gates behind, Francie and his friend took turns fighting me. They took turns because Francie wore glasses and needed someone to hold them while he was fighting. Somehow, we managed to end up outside the gate of Francie's home, which was some way from the school. As I think back on this, I am not at all sure how that happened. However, it was only the timely intervention of their family servant, who stopped the fight, that enabled me to survive that day to tell the story. After that fight, I was adamant that I would have nothing to do with my erstwhile friend. However, it was not long before Francie and I became best of friends again.

One day I overheard one of my teachers telling my mother that if I survived Kingsdale, which was a pretty rough environment in which to attend school, I would be 'set for life.'

That was not the only danger that I faced as a young schoolboy. One of the houses that I had to walk past to and from school had two big, noisy Dobermann Pinscher watch dogs. Every day, on my way past, they would jump up at the gate and bark and bare their teeth at me in a very threatening manner. I was very grateful that there was a secure gate and fence between us, and ever since, I have not liked the Dobermanns.

Francie was not my only friend. One of my other friends was a giant of a boy called Roy Fouche. I have a photo of the two of us, and another one of us with some other friends. He was so big that he looks as if he could have been my dad in the photo. Because he was so big, he was a great friend to have; however, he was a gentle giant and was never in fights at school or elsewhere. In fact, he was no real help to me in my fairly frequent battles, which usually took place just outside the school gates.

Despite anything that I have mentioned, my Junior School days were great. Over 60 years have passed since those days. Although I have not seen any of them, since 1957, or at the latest 1959, I have not forgotten my friends. They were Francie, his brother Cornie, Roy, his brother Bill, Richard Plain, David Dewie, Hendrik Pretorious, and Joan Bedingfield. Yes, Joan was the girl for me at junior School!

KINGSDALE JUNIOR SCHOOL DECEMBER 1956 HENDRICK PRETORIOUS, ROY FOUCHE, ALAN, FRANCIE, RONALD, & DAVID DEWIE. THE CHAP IN FRONT WAS OUR MASCOT!

FEDERATION

I mentioned how my friend Francie's family servant 'saved the day' when I was involved in that fight. Some people reading my story may think this to be rather strange, but it was customary for families to have a servant in those days. They needed the work, and most white families were happy to give them a job. Sadly, there was a great deal of racial prejudice around, and I grew up a racist like the rest of my friends.

One day I remember well was not long after the formation of 'The Federation of Rhodesia and Nyasaland' in 1953. Southern Rhodesia, a self-governing country by a white government since 1923, joined with the British Colonies, Northern Rhodesia and Nyasaland to form what proved to be a very successful Federation. On this particular day, I had gone to the bus stop on my bike to meet my mother as she returned from teaching at Marsicano School of Music. My mother used to catch the bus back from town, and I used to meet her and ride with her as she walked slowly back home. The bus used to terminate just outside Meldrum's General Store before returning to Bulawayo. There was a bench for people to sit on at the bus stop right outside the store, which had a sign painted on it that said very clearly, "WHITES ONLY."

When I arrived at the bus stop that afternoon, two black men were seated on the bench, and I, a boy of around ten years of age, asked them what they thought they were doing sitting on a bench reserved for white people. Instead of getting angry, they looked at each other and laughed and said, "Federation, Federation."

They were correct, the Federation did indeed

change some things, and it was a great success during the ten years that it existed. One of the things that it accomplished was to begin the long hard job of changing racial attitudes. As I look back at that incident, I am amazed at what I said to those men and their response, but strangely enough, I believe God began to change me that day, and as you will see, He continued that work later in South Africa.

CANCER

Sadly, my carefree life changed when my father was diagnosed with Lung Cancer. After suffering terribly for some months, my father died at the age of fifty on the 12th of April 1956. I was only 11 years old. He suffered terribly, and the intense pain was difficult for him to handle without medication. Even today, I can still smell the ointment that I used to rub on his arms and legs when he was in pain. Despite him suffering from lung cancer, he was a heavy smoker to the end, and I vowed that I would never smoke.

There was a large crowd of people at my father's funeral due to our large extended family in and around Bulawayo and his popularity at work, the Bulawayo Athletic Club and the different bars where he had worked. A service was held at the Methodist Church, followed by a short service at the grave side, but I do not remember much of that day. When the Methodist Minister came around to the house to arrange the funeral, he asked if anyone had a favourite hymn. When no one else responded, I requested *Abide With Me*, a hymn that I had come to love.

During the years that we knew our neighbour,

Mr. Pedder, my friend Dennis's father, he tried many different things to earn a living. I remember him being an insurance agent, running a chicken farm, and at this particular time working a gold mine. Like so many in the Bulawayo area, the mine was considered a 'small working.' When the gold-bearing ore came out of the ground, it was necessary to crush the rocks before the rest of the process could occur. Like most small workings, Mr. Pedder's had a three-stamp mill, which would pound the rock into the sand to extract the gold.

I mention our neighbors' gold mine because I spent some time on the mine after my father's funeral to help get my mind off my dad's death. It was fascinating to visit the mine, and Dennis, another chap and I had a great time getting thoroughly dirty swimming in the slime pits. At that time, they were not using Cyanide, a deadly poison, on the mine to extract the gold; otherwise, it would have been a very foolish thing to do!

As a result of my father's illness and death, I have always maintained that I grew up very quickly.

THE METHODIST CHURCH KINGSDALE.

There were no churches in the area where we lived when our house was built. Sometime before my father died, a Methodist Church was built in Kingsdale. Because some of our neighbours were Methodist, including the Pedders (Mr. Pedder was a Lay Preacher) and the Marriots who farmed nearby, they asked my mother if my sister and I would like to attend the Sunday School which we began to attend every Sunday. Until recently, I have always believed that my brothers never had the opportunity to attend Sunday School; however, I have discovered that they did attend, but I am not sure where. Nevertheless, I am so grateful for the wonderful opportunity to attend the Methodist Sunday School. It greatly influenced me and made my heart open to the Gospel in later years.

Sadly, my dad was what we used to call a 'Bush Baptist,' someone with no church ties. I believe their experience at the Dutch Reformed orphanage called 'Daisyfield,' near Bulawayo, put my dad and his brothers off religion. Regrettably, many people have been turned away from the Lord Jesus Christ by experiences that happened to them as children. What a tragedy that when they turn away from the visible church, they often permanently turn away from the Lord of Heaven and Earth, who is their only hope in this sin-sick world.

On the other hand, my mother had a Church of England background, but as there was no Anglican Church in the vicinity, she was happy that we went to the Methodist Church. I enjoyed Sunday School, and when they had a Family Service, I often brought my mother to the services. On one occasion, my eldest brother and one of his friends came along as well.

The friend was not used to church, and he asked if they had to pay to get in, and my brother, always a bit of a card, replied, "You do not pay to get in, but you have to pay to get out!"

We had no telephone, so when my father died late one night in Hospital, the hospital phoned a neighbour with the news. The neighbour was a qualified nurse and often came around to the house to give my father pain killer injections during his illness. I had often accompanied my mother late at night when she went around to ask her for help, which was not just next door but down the road.

On the night my father died, despite not hearing the neighbour's conversation when she came to the door with the news, I knew that he had died because The Lord told me what had happened while sleeping. In the morning, when my mother struggled to find the words to tell me that my father had died, I was able to tell her that I already knew as the Lord had told me. Praise God for that Methodist Church, as the Lord was at work in my life. My mother even told one of my teachers that I would be a minister one day. How prophetic was that?

I am not exactly sure and am entirely ignorant about why my family realised that I was the only one who had not been christened in the Anglican Church. It was most likely after my father died and before I went to boarding school. As a result, they decided, I am not sure they consulted me, that an 11-year-old boy called Alan Broadhurst Robertson would be Christened at St Johns Anglican Church in Bulawayo. I could go to the Methodist Sunday School, but I had to be 'christened' an Anglican!

For some reason, my family was no longer keen on the middle name 'Broadhurst,' registered at birth. It was a 'family name' adopted by many of the Robertson's and my father's middle name. As a result, there was some discussion over what to christen the youngest Robertson even though I had been Alan Broadhurst Robertson for 11 years. In these discussions, no one paid any attention to my suggestions, although it would be my name. The rest of the family decided that I should be Alan **David** Robertson even though Alan Broadhurst Robertson was on my birth certificate.

I was gutted that they did not consider my suggestions. I wanted to be known as Alan 'Roy Carson' (after all, didn't I have a grandmother who had been a **Carlsson**) or Alan 'Kit Rogers,' or Alan 'Bill Cassidy.' These were all the heroes of a comic mad youngster; however, no one listened. Even though I had been Tarzan mad sometime before, I must have gotten over it a little, as I do not remember asking to be called Alan **Tarzan** Robertson! And so, the day finally arrived, and I was duly christened in the Anglican Church as Alan David Robertson.

PLUMTREE HIGH SCHOOL

When my father died, I was in my last year at Junior School, my sister was at Eveline Girls High School in Bulawayo, and my eldest brother had only just left school. As already mentioned, he was working for an accountancy firm as an article clerk in Bulawayo. My other brother, Osmond, had just passed his Cambridge School Certificate and was planning to do his 'A' levels. After my father died, my mother realised that she could not afford to send both my brother, Osmond and me to boarding school at Plumtree, so she decided that I would have to go to a local Bulawayo secondary school.

Both my brothers were keen that I receive as good an education as they had received, so Osmond came up with another idea. Instead of continuing at school to do his 'A' levels, he left school to help my mother send me to boarding school. I only found out about this a few years ago, and I am so grateful for my brother's sacrifice on my behalf. My future could have been very different had I not had boarding school discipline after my father died.

As my grandfather and father were the second children in their families and had both died in their fifties, my brother Osmond, the second child of my mother and father, became a little concerned when approaching his fiftieth year. However, God has been good to him, and at the time of writing, he is over 80 years of age and doing quite well.

At the beginning of the school year, in January 1957, I boarded a special school train at Bulawayo Station bound for Plumtree. Plumtree is a tiny town some 60 miles from Bulawayo, near the border with Bechuanaland, now known as Botswana. Like my brothers before me, I was assigned to Lloyd House, one of four 'Houses' at a school of around 300 male students. In 1957, Lloyd House had won the School Sports every year for some years. I began my senior school career as a somewhat overweight 12-year-old, but I was slim and trimmed within one school term.

I believe the two main reasons for losing weight during my first term at Plumtree were not eating my mother's home cooking, and possibly, the main reason, every afternoon we had athletics, like it or not. We were in serious training for the school sports. You name it; we did it, 100yds, 400yds, 800yds, javelin, shot-put, discus, high jump, long jump, and cross country. I was in 'Lloyd,' and we had won the school sports for some years in a row and the plan was to win it again at all costs!

I remember one particular cross country training session well. As usual, I was bringing up the rear (someone has to look after the stragglers) and fell a considerable distance behind. Nevertheless, as we approached the finishing line, I decided to give it a bit of a spurt, even though it was a long time since the leaders had come in, and as I arrived at the finishing line, I was given a standing ovation. Needless to say, they did not pick me to represent our house at the school sports. Despite my poor performance, during my three years at Plumtree, Lloyd House continued to win the school sports. I have discovered, the year after I left, Lloyd House failed to win the athletics, sadly, which remained the case for some years.

Getting back to the food, it was not the best by any means. The boys went on strike, refusing to eat the food that dished up to us for lunch. When we arrived for our supper, they dished the same food that we had refused to eat at lunch. The strike did not last long as we were all too hungry. A story went around that a donkey cart used to arrive at the kitchen with two donkeys, and it would leave with one. The other donkey was butchered and made into the mince that we were eating. Whatever the reason, Alan Robertson began his school career at Plumtree as a rather plump schoolboy but quickly became a much trimmer specimen.

Plumtree High School was an all-white boys' school, and so it was quite an event when we had the visit from a black athlete from the USA somewhere between 1957 and 1959. On that occasion, we were all required to go up to the sports field, where he showed us his abilities by taking on our best school athletes.

THE ATHELETE FROM THE USA

All of the white boys' schools in Southern Rhodesia in those days would have had a Cadet Force, and Plumtree was no exception. All the older boys were required to be involved with the cadets unless medically exempt. I am sure that I was involved before leaving to go to South Africa.

Excelling in school sports was not the only thing to occupy our 'spare time' during that first term. Mrs. Turner, the house master's wife, was very keen on amateur dramatics, and she, supported by the rest of the staff, produced a Gilbert and Sullivan Musical. During the second, or Winter term, it was a play by William Shakespeare. I played in *The Pirates of Penzance, The Mikado*, and maybe another production, but I cannot remember it.

Sadly, I was not a pirate in *The Pirates of Penzance.* Much to my disgust, many of my friends and I ended up in the chorus line dressed as girls, which was very embarrassing for me. So, one Christmas holiday, I made sure that when I returned to school with a 'crew-cut.' Despite my very short hair, some lady still managed to put a curl in my hair so that I fitted the part a little better!

**PIRATES OF PENZANCE CHORUS LINE.
ALAN SECOND ROW, FIFTH FROM THE LEFT.**

Now, you probably will have guessed that the reason my mother went to such expense to send me to Plumtree was not so that I could come near the back in the cross country, or indeed appear in the chorus line in *The Pirates of Penzance,* it was so that I could be educated! So, what happened in this area of my life at boarding school?

On the academic side, because I had come second in

class at Kingsdale, I was placed in the 'A' stream during that first term, meaning that I experienced Latin's intricacies with all the other bright students. However, at the end of the first term, they made a little adjustment and reassigned me to the 'B' stream. As a 'B' stream student, I did not have to bother with Latin and was amongst the less intellectual students. We would write our Cambridge School Certificate in five years instead of four. As Kingsdale was a tiny school, coming second in class out of around six was not such a big deal!

Having told you the story of my valiant effort to protect a younger student from bullying by two older boys at Junior School, I have sadly to tell you about my shameful bullying of a student at Senior School. It is not something that I am proud of, and it went against everything that my family stood for, but it is part of my story. Praise God that when I finally invited Jesus into my life, He changed me!

My two brothers had been at Plumtree (the best boy's school in the land) shortly before me and had both been very well-liked. Osmond was so popular that some seniors in Lloyd called me Ossie after my brother.

During long weekend holidays like 'Easter,' and 'Rhodes and Founders,' some boys could not return home as it was too far. Many lived in Mashonaland, on the other side of the country. They would spend the holiday weekend at school, or friends who lived around Bulawayo would sometimes invite them to spend the weekend with them.

My eldest brother had two good friends, who were twins, and they spent some weekends visiting us while they were at Plumtree. The twins had a brother my age, and everyone hoped that we, too, would be firm friends when we went to boarding school. However, when we arrived at school, I had other ideas and spurned his hand of friendship favouring other boys. In fact, over time, instead of befriending him, I began to bully him. One evening, between our evening meal and prep, he forcibly objected to my bullying. I told him that we could always fight if he didn't like it. You may remember that I had had a lot of experience in that area, and with all the cross-country training, I was in top form.

To my surprise, when I suggested that we fight, he agreed! I suppose because I had caused him such a lot of pain, he was sick of being bullied and wanted a chance to get his own back. Once we began to fight, it was not long before I had him on the ground, advising him to give in, but he refused! I must have been distracted, and suddenly, he was on top of me. He was not in the mood for a chat and did not offer me terms of peace but hit me as hard as he could. Who knows how the fight would have ended, but just then, the bell went for prep, and the battle was over? This fight was my last physical fight, and it was a fight that I lost. I deserved everything that I received, and if by some miracle this is read by Hamish Stewart, I am deeply sorry for how I treated you. Please forgive me!!

On some weekends we were given a day pass and a packed lunch and allowed to explore the surrounding countryside. Some of my friends were keen collectors of birds' eggs and possessed extensive collections. I learned a lot from them. For example, I learned not to take all the eggs from the nest but always to leave at least one. I also learned how to blow the egg to get the yoke and white out so that you can keep the egg in your collection. Besides, I discovered that snakes were also after birds' eggs, and we had to be on the lookout as there were quite a few around. The 'kopjies,' or rocky granite hills, were wonderful places to explore.

I cannot forget one event that took place during my first year at Plumtree. On the 4th of October 1957, the Soviet Union launched the World's first satellite. It orbited the earth for three weeks before its batteries died, and then, two months later, it fell back to earth. One night, most likely, on a Saturday before the weekly film show, we gathered outside the Beit Hall and looked up into the sky as *Sputnik 1* passed overhead. We were all amazed that such a thing should occur and that we could look up into the night sky and see it pass overhead.

On Sunday mornings, we were all required to attend Chapel, which I was happy to do. The School Chaplin, the local Anglican minister, ran the chapel. I had a very healthy respect for God. I sometimes attended the Christian Union, mainly when they showed Moody Science Films that I thoroughly enjoyed, but that is about as far as things went spiritually while I was at Plumtree.

THE CHAPEL AT PLUMTREE.

Although Plumtree school was a government boarding school, it had been established and was always run on British public-school lines. As a new boy in 1957, I was assigned as the 'fag' or servant to one of the prefects. I ended up being the 'fag' of Harold Meldrum, who lived near our home in Bulawayo. Some years earlier, he visited our home to speak with brothers about what to expect at Plumtree before going as a 'new boy'. Now, he was a prefect, and I was the 'new boy' and his 'fag'.

As there were a lot of new boys that year in Lloyd House, he ended up having four 'fags' and did not know what to do with us. Nevertheless, he did his best, and I got the job of checking his timetable and taking all his books to the prefects' common room every day, before school. Sadly, I was not too good at the job, resulting in Harold having Geography notes in his Science notebook and History notes in his English notebook, and so on. One day, he decided that things had to change!

I was not the only one who was failing to do his job correctly. The 'fag' responsible for putting down his mosquito net at night was also failing, while the 'fag' responsible for cleaning his study had not come up to scratch either! As a result, he called us all in, used his big 'takkie' (running shoe), and applied it to our rear ends. 'Fag' number four had not failed, but for good measure, he had the 'takkie' applied to his rear end too. I suppose it must have worked as I believe that his notes were in the right books the rest of the year! Sadly, I understand that Harold died some years ago, or else I would apologise to him as well as to Hamish!

LLOYD HOUSE 1958
ALAN, THIRD ROW, SECOND FROM THE RIGHT.

WEDDINGS IN THE FAMILY

The year 1959 turned out to be very important in our family. Osmond married Colleen Robinson on the 30th June 1959, and my mother married Fred Tilliduff from Cape Town in South Africa that same year.

After the church service, my mother and Uncle Fred had a reception somewhere in Bulawayo. Sadly, I consumed a significant amount of alcohol, partly with the assistance of a couple of my uncles who were working behind the bar.

Before the evening was over, to my shame, I was very drunk. I overheard someone say, "If that was my so…."

The school allowed me time off to attend the wedding, and I stayed a few nights with the Marriot's on their farm. As a result of my overindulgence at the wedding reception, I was very sick the following day. However, they looked after me well, and their daughter, Roseanne, took me horse riding around the farm, which I enjoyed.

I returned to Plumtree to finish the academic year before sadly saying goodbye, to a great school and great friends. They were Jonny Johnson (he had another name, which I learned after spending a few days at his parent's farm, but I had to swear never to repeat it at school), Ian Paper, Charlie Piers, Brian Cummings, and many others. I was also sad because I had been looking forward to having 'fags' of my own, and moving away at that time denied me the privilege. Still, as you will discover, God had other plans that involved me moving a long way from home. Sadly, our family home at 11 Orange Grove in Bulawayo was no more, and our family was scattered. My mother and her four children would never all be together, in the same place again. My sister, two brothers and I would only ever be together once more in our entire lives when my brother Christopher arranged a reunion over 50 years later.

It is hard to believe, but the next time my two brothers, sister and I, would all be together, in the same place, would be in Bristol, England, in 2011, 52 years later. Three of us have been together on one or two occasions, two of us have been together on many occasions, but that was the only occasion we were all four together.

Strangely, I had broached the idea in 1994 when I was about to turn 50, but no one seemed to be interested. Anyhow, when my eldest brother (seniority counts) felt a need to have a family reunion, we all responded positively, and it was amazing that we could all be present. My sister and husband travelled from Canada, Osmond came on his own from South Africa, and I travelled alone down from Preston in Lancashire to Bristol. I am so grateful to Christopher for arranging that reunion, as it would not have been possible at any time since then, as so much has changed.

Chapter 2

CAPE TOWN

I saw the academic year out in Rhodesia, and at the end of 1959, I travelled down to Cape Town in South Africa by train (a journey of around 1000 miles from Bulawayo) to live with my mother and stepfather. We agreed I would call my stepfather Uncle Fred, so I will call him that throughout this book. Avril came a little later to live with us. She did a secretarial course in Cape Town but returned to Bulawayo in Rhodesia as soon as she could.

Uncle Fred had two children by his first marriage, Daphne, married with a family, and Malcolm, who was still single in 1959. Like his father before him, Malcolm became a Jehovah's Witness, although Uncle Fred had left the JW's many years before.

SOUTH AFRICAN COLLEGE SCHOOL (SACS)

As I look back upon my life, I am very grateful to my mother and Uncle Fred for enrolling me at SACS, one of the best schools in Cape Town at the time. The South African College School (SACS) was founded in September 1829, and it is the oldest High School in South Africa. Cape Town University was established from this school.

In 1960, when I enrolled at SACS, the school was situated in 'The Gardens' right in the centre of Cape Town. However, it was due to relocate to Newlands later that year, where they had acquired a fabulous piece of land at the foot of the mountains. 'The Gardens' were initially created in 1652 when Jan Van Riebeeck landed at the Cape. He established a fruit and vegetable garden, where ships of the Dutch East India Company could stock up with fresh produce on their way to the East Indies. In 1960, many people enjoyed a lovely park, every day, right in the City's centre.

My school journey started each morning when Uncle Fred dropped me off on his way to work at Rondebosch train station. From there, I caught the suburban train into the centre of Cape Town and then walked a short distance along Adderley Street to 'The Gardens'. The final part of my journey was through this beautiful park to the school gates. On the way home, I would reverse the trip but would catch a bus home from the station instead of going with Uncle Fred. I count it such a privilege to have attended SACS in their old premises for a short time before moving in 1960.

The new school was in Newlands, not far from where we lived in Rondebosch, so I could now cycle to school, instead of using public transport. The new school buildings and playing fields were spectacular, situated at the foot of Table Mountain and Devils Peak. A shortcut going to and from the school led down a steep road that joined a very busy road at the bottom of the hill. There were occasions when I had to use all the skills I had learned as a kid, as my brakes were not up to scratch, especially with the weight of a passenger and myself down a very steep road.

At SACS, I first remember being called AB, in this case, spelt Abe, by one of my friends. Many Jewish boys attended the school, resulting in some of the other students believing that I must also be Jewish. (Abe, my boy.) Still, the nickname never really stuck, and it was several years later when I came to be known by my initials as AB.

Moving from Plumtree to SACS created a problem as the Cape Province's academic year was very different from Rhodesia's. The school year in Cape Town commenced in September, the same as the school year in Britain, and I had arrived very near the end of two years of preparation for an external exam known as Junior Certificate, which was taken at the end of the third year, or Standard 8 at SACS. The head Master felt that if they put me in standard 8, which was equivalent to our third year at Plumtree, I would fail, as I would have less than six months to cover the two-year course for an external exam. In their wisdom, they put me in standard 7, a year below my age group. How sad is that?

Besides, if you recall, I had started my school year at Plumtree in the 'A' stream until they realised their mistake and put me in the 'B' stream. However, at SACS, the system was a little different, and as the school had many more students, they had four standard seven classes. I was in 'B4', which was naturally even more upsetting as the equivalent would have been a 'D' stream at Plumtree!

However, on a brighter note, in that 1960 school year in Cape Town, my teachers naturally recognised my abilities and thought that I would sail through the standard seven exams! I also thought that it would be no problem for me, as I was now two grades below my friends back at Plumtree. Sadly, my teachers, parents, and I were shocked when I failed standard seven a few months later. It was an enormous shock to the system. I was furious and humiliated to have to repeat standard seven. However, I showed great diligence over the next two years, passed standard 7, and received my Junior Certificate in June 1962.

Now, before we leave the classroom, there is one story that I feel that I must share. At SACS, I was privileged to do 'Business Studies,' and the instruction that I received has been a blessing to me right through my life. We had an excellent teacher, but sadly, he had a drinking problem. He would need a drink every so often, and by the end of the school day, he was not up to much.

Many years before, he had produced a series of test papers and continued to use them year after year instead of creating new ones. The students knew this and acquired past test papers and even wrote the test before it happened. They would then smuggle them into the classroom and replace the examination of the day. The teacher, well aware of what was happening, was happy for the end-of-year exams to sort out the cheaters from those who had worked all year!

Well, on one occasion after a test, in which I had received good marks, assuming that I had cheated - which really annoyed me, he said, "If you get marks like that at the end of year exams, I will buy you a farm in Adderley Street!"

Well, I did get marks equally as good when I wrote my Junior Certificate exams, but because I left the school before the results came out, I failed to get my farm in the middle of Adderley Street in Cape Town! Anyhow, even if I had reminded him of what he had said, he had never mentioned what type of farm he was considering in Adderley Street! We need to remember that Adderley Street was right in the centre of Cape Town, so maybe he had a 'Flea Farm' in mind!

It was wonderful living in Cape Town, as it is a beautiful city! Wherever you are in Cape Town, Table Mountain, or one of the other mountains is never far away, so it is not surprising that they had a Mountain Club at SACS, which I was encouraged to join. The teacher in charge, Mr. Basson, was a great instructor and much of what he taught us about being on the mountainside, I have never forgotten. We never did any serious mountaineering but used the many different easy routes like Skeleton Gorge, Platteklip Gorge, and Nursery Ravine.

On one occasion, the Mountain Club, led by Mr. Basson, went on a camping trip for a week in the Cederberg mountains around 180 miles from Cape Town. It was truly amazing hiking in the mountains and seeing so much of God's beautiful creation. It was there that I learned the joy of having Koo Apricot Jam on Cheddar Cheese.

CAMPING IN THE MOUNTAINS.

ALAN IS NEXT TO A DONKEY ON THE LEFT

Two of the easy routes up Table Mountain started

in Kirstenbosch National Botanical Gardens, another wonderful place to visit. I was extremely privileged to be part of the Mountain Club as the outings were great fun, and I learnt much from those experiences. As a result of my experience, while living in Cape Town, I led a friend, a born 'Capetonian' up Table Mountain, which he had never done before.

LIVING IN CAPE TOWN

As I have already mentioned, living in Cape Town was a real blessing as it is one of the most beautiful cities in the world. Amazing beaches were not far away, such as Fish Hoek, Muizenberg, Hout Bay, or one of the other places on the coast where there was great swimming. The waves at Muizenberg were fantastic for surfing with or without a surfboard, and although we did not get to the beach very often, we enjoyed it when we did.

Although we lived in Rondebosch (which was considered a very good address in Cape Town), our immediate neighbours, Mr. and Mrs. Pratt, lived in Claremont. They had two daughters, Norma and Margaret, and a son I am not sure that I ever met. Their daughter, Margaret, was a similar age to me, and the son and Norma were a good deal older, children from Mr. Pratt's first marriage. The Pratts were Churchgoers and sought a meaningful relationship with the Lord. They did some heart-searching as to where they should go to church. In time, this search led them to the Assembly of God, but that comes much later in my story.

There were several young people my age on our street, and I soon made good friends. The Bennet's, who lived at the end of the street, had a daughter, Vivian, and a younger son called Christopher. One evening I was the first to arrive at a birthday party held for Vivian at their home. I could hear that there was a fair bit of panic when I knocked on the door, as I was a little early, but when they discovered that it was me, and not the latest boyfriend, I heard, most likely Mrs. Bennet, exclaim, "It's only, Alan!" With that, the panic ended!

The main reason that I mention the family was because of Christopher. He was, without doubt, the naughtiest boy that I had ever met up and till then. The entire street complained about Christopher, but his mother would not believe that her little angel would do any of the things they accused him of doing. However, God is so good. Many years later, I came across Christopher, and he was a dedicated born-again believer in fellowship with a local church. When Christopher told me who he was and that he was now a born-again believer, I said that if God could save him, he could, without a doubt, save anyone. It was lovely to see this young man serving Jesus when he could so easily have gone the other way.

A Jewish family lived across the road, and their son, Ivan, and another boy who lived next door to Ivan, and I, became firm friends. Mr. Kessel, Ivan's father, had a fishing boat, and every Sunday, they would go fishing. They often asked if I wanted to join them on a Sunday, but I was going to be confirmed and had committed to being in the morning service every Sunday, so I never went. Nevertheless, after I was confirmed (more about that later), I spent an enjoyable day fishing from their boat in the sea off Gordon's Bay.

The other boy, whose name I cannot remember, had a coin collection, and as I also collected coins, we spent some enjoyable time together. We were able to look at coins from all around the world. I was amazed to see the wad of German Marks his father had given to him, with the values of millions of Marks on each note. When the German Currency had devalued so fast, the banknotes became worthless. I was happy to receive a few of these banknotes at the time, never realising that a similar thing would happen in my homeland of Zimbabwe many years later.

THIRTY THOUSAND MARCH ON CAPE TOWN

In 1948 the Nationalist party won the national elections for the first time in South Africa. They implemented a 'Separate Development' policy for the different racial groups in the country, better known by Afrikaans name, 'Apartheid!' To implement this policy, amongst other things, they introduced and enforced the 'Pass Laws,' seriously hindering the freedom of movement of the black and coloured (an acceptable name for the mixed race) population of South Africa.

To make their voice heard, the leader of the Pan-African Congress organised a march of protest against the existence of these laws. He managed to mobilise between thirty and fifty thousand Black South Africans from the Township of Langa. They marched to the Caledon Square Police Station in the centre of Cape Town on the 30th March 1960, determined to put their case to the Minister of Justice.

I was at school in Newlands, and we were all sent home for fear that violence would erupt. Sometime later, I discovered that a huge number of black workers had advanced on the centre of Cape Town, demanding to speak to the Minister of Justice. He had stated that he would not negotiate with a mob, but he would meet with them if the leaders sent the crowds home. The leaders agreed and sent their supporters home, and the Minister of Justice arrested the leaders and had them all put in prison.

I have verified most of this story, and as a young man, I was horrified to hear what had happened. I had always understood that a 'White Man' was a man of his word, and if he said something, then he would do it. I could not understand how the Minister of Justice could make a promise and then break it when the others had done what he asked them to do. This incident significantly impacted my thinking; God was changing this racist young schoolboy, and I am so glad that He was.

THE SCHOOLS AND VARSITY CAMP

I was privileged to go on a Schools and Varsity Christian Camp during one of the school holidays. We travelled by train from Cape Town to the venue some distance away but cannot remember how we got from the station to the campground. We stayed in dormitory-type buildings, right on the coast, in a beautiful area of the Cape Province. Each day was filled with activities, both physical and spiritual. On one memorable occasion, we went for a hike up the coast, past a cliff above the beach. On the way back, instead of following the hike's leaders, I decided to follow some other guys, who were taking a shortcut to the beach, by climbing down the cliff. Anyhow, I ran into a problem, as some way down the cliff, I could not find a handhold or a foothold anywhere! I was in serious trouble, as I was trapped, high above the beach, with jagged rocks below, and nowhere to go.

It was then that I prayed, and I am pretty confident it was the first time that I knew that God had answered my prayer. Immediately after I prayed, I discovered a foothold and then a handhold, and as a result, I was finally able to climb down and onto the beach. I do not doubt that the Lord saved me from a serious accident that day. Praise God; He does answer prayer!

Every evening after supper, we gathered together for a meeting on the spiritual side and sang hymns and gospel songs, and I think someone preached, but I really cannot remember. One of the songs that touched my heart during the week, which I have never forgotten, was the old hymn *When The Roll Is Called Up Yonder*. Sadly, although my heart was open to the Lord, I could not confidently say "I'll be there" with the songwriter. I was not quite there, and it would need something else to bring me into the right relationship with God.

'YOUTH FOR CHRIST'

Sometime after this, 'Youth For Christ' held a Crusade in our area, in the local scout hall. I would not have known about it, but Margaret, my neighbour, and a few of her friends invited me to attend with them. It was just what I needed, and that night, I decided to follow Christ.

My decision for Christ was so real that it felt as if there was no pavement beneath my feet after the meeting when I walked home that night. I knew that I was 'saved' and that Jesus had come into my life. That night, I could easily have sung that old hymn, *When The Roll Is Called Up Yonder,* and confidently have said, "I'll be there." I knew that the Lord Jesus had come into my life. It was so genuine. God was real; Jesus had come into my life! Sadly, I was the only one from our party who responded to the Gospel that night.

After the meeting, one of the local 'Youth For Christ' workers did his very best to follow up on me. Sadly, despite what had taken place, I was not all that responsive and only went to one or two of their meetings. He is another one of those individuals that I should apologise to, as he tried so hard with little success. Be that as it may, the Lord had done a genuine work in my life, and God was not going to give up on me, as the rest of my story will confirm.

MY ANGLICAN CONFIRMATION

Around this time, I decided to be confirmed in the Anglican Church; I am sure that it was my decision, not my parents. I joined a group of between 6 and 10 young people taking confirmation classes at the local church. Sad to say, I was the only one who was there because I wanted to be confirmed. Most, if not all the others, were there because their parents had sent them along - so that they would be able to get married in the Anglican Church.

The Vicar, who led the classes at St. Saviours Church in Claremont, was a sincere man. At his suggestion, I religiously attended the early morning Holy Communion service every Sunday. I received a lot from those services, and I can remember waiting expectantly every Sunday for the following words to be read out during the service as they touched my heart, "...and the peace of God, which surpasses all understanding, will guard your hearts and minds through Jesus Christ." Philippians 4.7

The Vicar rightly encouraged us to get a Bible because how can you get to know God unless you are willing to read His Word? However, he also instructed us to make sure that it included the Apocrypha, which was not good advice!

The Archbishop of Cape Town, no less, confirmed me. My mother and Uncle Fred presented me with a wonderful gift, a lovely Bible. However, I made sure that I checked to see if it had the Apocrypha. When I found that it did not include the Apocrypha, I asked if I could change it. They did as I asked, and I received what I asked for, but it was nowhere near as good as the Bible that I had turned down. Sadly, the advice that this very genuine man gave me was misguided.

Let me make it very clear; you do not need to have the Apocrypha in your Bible, as the books included in the Apocrypha are not accepted as the Word of God by most Bible-believing Christians. They may be worth reading, but are not accepted as the undefiled Word of God! It will take you a lifetime to get to know the Bible well, which has 66 Books without the Apocrypha.

FAMILY VISITS

I want to relate two visits by family members to you. The first was a visit from my brother, Christopher. I cannot remember much about his visit; however, I remember what he asked me to do before he arrived. The MCC (Middlesex Cricket Club) visited South Africa around

1960-61 and were due to play at Newlands Cricket Grounds against the Cape Province team. Christopher asked me to get tickets for him and a friend as they wanted to see the match. I needed to queue all night outside the grounds if I hoped to get a ticket in the morning, so, accompanied by two friends mentioned, I camped outside the Newlands Cricket Grounds to purchase tickets for a game that I would not attend. I do not remember my brother offering a reward, but possibly we did it just for the fun of it.

The other visit was from my cousin Mary Robertson, Uncle Noel's daughter. As we were sitting on the small porch outside our house in Rondebosch, she lit a cigarette and asked whether I had started smoking. My reply was that I had not begun smoking and had no intention of ever smoking in my life. She did not believe what I had said and offered me a bet that I would have started smoking before turning 21 years of age. We shook hands on the bet and agreed on a small monetary figure. Some years later, when I turned 21 and had not started smoking, and I never have, I made sure that I contacted her and reminded her of our bet; however, I didn't ask her to pay up!

BOARDING SCHOOL AGAIN

My mother longed for the simpler lifestyle that she had known in Rhodesia, never really settling in Cape Town, so Uncle Fred, to his credit, looked for work in Rhodesia to please my mother. He secured a position as Works Manager with British Cellophane, who had recently opened a factory in Salisbury, so they packed up the house and moved.

Sadly, this was only a few months before I was due to write my exams, and I needed to get my Junior Certificate before leaving. As the job could not wait, I ended up boarding at SACS for my final term. The hostel was much more modern than Lloyd House at Plumtree, as it had only been constructed a couple of years earlier. Instead of a dormitory with around 30 boys, I was in a dormitory with only six beds. To my surprise, I soon discovered that three of the boys were committed, born-again believers, just like myself, and we were all members of the Anglican Church. As I look back upon this, I am genuinely amazed at the goodness of God. He was certainly looking after me. Hallelujah!

I think it must have been because of these other believers that I ended up going to the youth group at St. Saviours Church in Claremont, where I was confirmed! One evening I was privileged to attend an exciting event led by the Youth Leader. We were put in different teams and travelled all around town by car (not the whole of Cape Town), following clues hidden at various points along the journey. One of the older boys who may have been the Youth Leader, whose brother was at Theological College studying for the ministry, was particularly good to me. He made a great impression upon me as a young Christian, an excellent example of a man dedicated to the Lord. Sadly, I have forgotten his name.

When we discovered that four of us were 'born-again' believers in the dormitory, I suggested we organise a regular prayer meeting. The others agreed, so we met together to pray. Although I had made the suggestion, I do not think that I had ever prayed in public before. The other boys expectantly waited for me to lead them in prayer on the first day that we met. Eventually, one of the boys said that I should lead in prayer as it was my suggestion. Well, having been so challenged, I did. It was a very short prayer and not at all what they had expected! However, after a shaky start, I believe we continued to meet for prayer regularly.

MY WORKING HOLIDAY

All too soon, the day arrived for me to leave SACS, but my parents had arranged one last treat before leaving the Cape. A good friend of Uncle Fred, Joe Armstrong, was the harbour Master in Cape Town, and he arranged for me to travel up the west coast to Walvis Bay in South West Africa. It would be a working holiday. I would assist the crew whilst on board. It turned out that I only did minimal work. The holiday part was fantastic.

South West Africa, previously part of the German Empire from 1884 until 1915 due 'The Scramble for Africa,' was now under the administration of South Africa. During the 1st World War, it was conquered by South African and British forces. The Union of South Africa took over administration until it became independent, becoming Namibia on the 21st March 1990.

Returning to my story, after an evening out with the Youth Group, they dropped me off at the harbour gates at around 9.00 pm, the night before we were due to sail. I walked through the harbour to where the ship was moored; we were scheduled to leave very early the next morning. The harbour was deserted with shadows everywhere, and to be quite honest, it was a little scary, so I was pleased when I was finally aboard. A young seaman, a little older than myself, made me very welcome, took care of me, and showed me the ropes.

It was a great trip with the ship calling at several different places along the west coast of South Africa and South West Africa, including Lüderitz. We were unable to dock, so we unloaded into smaller boats that came alongside the ship. My main job was to keep an eye open for anything unusual when the men were loading and unloading.

We finally arrived at Walvis Bay, our destination and last port of call. Some of the crew asked if I wanted to travel to Swakopmund, a town a little further up the coast. I jumped at the chance and enjoyed the journey as we travelled alongside the desert (a lot of SWA is desert) until we came to a small coastal town. The thing that caught my eye was the wonderful palm tree-covered beach, which looked refreshing after the arid desert we had just traveled alongside. I thoroughly enjoyed the outing, but sadly, we could not stay very long before we had to return. I must admit that I had never seen or have still not seen a beach as lovely as I saw at Swakopmund that day. I would say it would take a lot of beating.

Back in Walvis Bay, I was introduced to the Seaman's Mission by my young friend, where we were warmly received and played table tennis, darts, and billiards or pool. It was a great place to go, and over the years, many men have been encouraged knowing that there are Christian believers concerned for the welfare of seafaring men.

It was soon time to return to Cape Town, and the return journey was as enjoyable. Once I returned, it was time to catch the train to Salisbury in Southern Rhodesia. This time the train journey was a little longer, more like 1500 miles, but I have no recollection of the trip. Praise

God; I was going home!

Chapter 3

SALISBURY

THE QUEENS HOTEL.

I arrived in Salisbury in June/July 1962. My mother and Uncle Fred had still not found a suitable house to rent. While looking for a house, we all stayed at the Queens Hotel at the top of Manica Road in Salisbury. Mrs. Frick, the receptionist, also lived in the hotel with her husband and two sons, Helge Schneemann (my spelling may be wrong) and his half-brother Ronnie Frick. They had recently moved from Tanganyika and lived some years in Rhodesia before finally moving to South Africa.

As Helge and I were around the same age and living in the hotel, we spent quite a lot of time together and became good friends. One night we watched a War film on TV, and having witnessed some of the terrible atrocities that were committed by the Nazis during the war, as portrayed by the film, Helge turned to me and said, "I am ashamed to be German!"

He was ashamed to be a German because of all the terrible crimes that the Nazi regime under Hitler had perpetrated. I responded by assuring him that it was not his fault, as he had not even been born until after the war ended, and what his countrymen had done during the Second World War had nothing to do with him. I then assured him that what was more important was what he did with his own life, not what others had done before he was born.

Although I was a Christian at that time, having

only recently responded to the claims of Christ upon my life, I failed to take the opportunity to speak to him about Jesus. Sadly, I was no longer in fellowship with other believers and was already beginning to drift away.

STORTFORD

The day finally arrived when we moved into a rented house some 7 miles from Salisbury's center on the Old Gatooma Road. We had to drive out of Salisbury on a full tarmac road to get there, past the turn-off to Mabelreign, until we came to the turn-off for the Mabelreign Drive-In Cinema. At that point, the road changed to a strip road, which we followed, until we reached our turn off onto a dirt road.

The 'strips' had been laid during the depression in the '30s to employ out-of-work Europeans to open up the country. The idea was that you drove with your tyres on each strip and got off one of the strips when there was an oncoming car so that you each had one strip to drive on. By the time we moved into the area, many of these strip roads had already been replaced by full tarmac roads. Others had been converted into narrow tarmac roads by filling in the middle section. This stretch of road remained a strip road for some years after 1962, when we moved into the area.

The property was called Stortford, and the house was on around 50 acres of land. There was a plantation of Gum Trees on a large portion of the land. The house had two rondavels, one at either end of a modest veranda. The rondavels were constructed in the same way as the tribal African houses using 'pole and dagga' (poles and mud) and then painted over with lime wash.

The rest of the house was equally quaint with a 'Rhodesian boiler' outside the back which provided hot water effectively. It was constructed out of a 44-gallon oil drum, with a wood fire placed underneath.

STORTFORD WITH MY MOTHER AND UNCLE FRED.

THE COLLAPSE OF A RONDAVEL AT STORTFORD. ALAN, THE DOGS, JESSIE, & OSMOND AND DOROTHY BOYES.

During most of our time at Stortford we had a servant named California, who had a very good sense of humour and was a hard worker. California was not his real name, but an adopted name that we could pronounce, as most people from an English background are not good at learning foreign languages and are never good at pronouncing the local names. He lived on the property with his wife, who was a simple woman.

One of the stories that I have to tell about California took place during my last year at school. One of my school friends' father was a joiner by trade, and he had built some lovely cabinets for radios and record players. He had not managed to sell all of them, and when I saw them in his garage, I was most impressed. My friend asked his father, on my behalf, if I could have one, and he agreed. I cannot remember if I paid for it.

Uncle Fred agreed to pick up one of these beautiful pieces of furniture for me. When we arrived home, California helped me carry it into my bedroom (one of the Rondavels) and burst out laughing. The reason for his mirth was my new item of furniture. It was lovely to look at as it had a highly polished surface; however, he had noticed the open back, and could not stop laughing. It was great on the outside but not at all right on the inside. There is a message there for all of us!

As the driver at his work was having difficulty finding somewhere to live in Salisbury, Uncle Fred allowed him to live on the property with his wife and child, as California and his wife only occupied half of the servants' quarters.

FINISHING SCHOOL

Although I had finally achieved a reasonably good Junior Certificate at SACS, my education was far from complete. As a result, I soon enrolled at Ellis Robins Boys School in Mabelreign, the closest Senior School to where we lived. I have always said that I went to the best school in Rhodesia, Plumtree; then we moved to Cape Town, and I enrolled in one of the best schools in the area, SACS; finally, I went to 'Finishing School' at Ellis Robins in Mabelreign. Although it was not among the 'best', I have no regrets about my time at Ellis Robins!

For the first week, or it may have been longer, Uncle Fred would drop me off at school on his way to work, which was usually very early. But, after school, I had to make my own way home, which was quite a walk, as I had yet to discover the shortcut. Although school finished at 1.00 pm, I would only arrive home at around 3.00 pm. Thankfully, it wasn't long before I had a new bicycle (which had a bell, brakes and mudguards) making the journey to and from school much quicker. Because I had 'wheels', I was also able to explore and discovered a perfect shortcut. In time I had it down to a fine art; it took around 15 minutes to get to school, and usually, I would be cycling past the school to the entrance, just as the bell started ringing for the start of the school day.

It is sobering to note that when I started school as a child, I was the youngest in my class, and by the time I arrived at Ellis Robins and was finally preparing for the Cambridge School Certificate, I was the oldest in my class. Still, I am pleased to report that we had an excellent History teacher who did his best to encourage all his students to do well at school. I remember him telling us that the African students (we considered ourselves to be Europeans) were eager to learn and that things would change in Rhodesia in time. It would be wise to have a good education. Sadly, few bothered to pay attention to what he was saying.

Our English Literature teacher was excellent, and she really brought lessons to life. Although I do not remember the poem that she taught us, I have never forgotten the first line, "Do You Remember an Inn, Miranda?"

With the internet's help, I discovered that this line of poetry came from a poem called *Tarantella*, written by Hilaire Belloc in 1929. I didn't remember the rest of the poem as I was much more interested in prose than poetry, and I remember a remarkable short story that she read to us called *Ichabod*.

The story was about a gentleman who travelled

the world over many years with his battered suitcase, plastered with stickers, telling all and sundry where he had been. Sadly, his suitcase went missing on one journey, and to his delight, he finally traced it to a lost property office. When he retrieved his suitcase, the kindly clerk mentioned that he had cleaned it up for him while it was in his care. When he saw his suitcase, he cried out, *Ichabod*. The many stickers to tell of all his travels had vanished; in fact, the glory has departed!

If you are reading my story and do not know the Bible story about a newborn child named 'Ichabod' by his dying mother, you need to check it out in the Bible. The Bible tells us that a war was taking place between Israel and the neighbouring Philistines. Someone suggested that if they took the 'Ark of the Covenant,' which spoke of God's presence, into the battle with them, then God would enable the Israelites to achieve victory. Eli's wicked sons, Hophni and Phineas, agreed to carry the Ark into battle. The Lord allowed the Philistines to defeat the Israelites, killing the two priests and capturing the Ark. Eli was so shocked that he fell off the bench that he was sitting on and died. When his daughter-in-law heard the news, she went into labour, and named her son Ichabod because the glory had departed from Israel, the Philistines had captured the Ark of God!

At the end of 1963, I was thrilled to get a good Cambridge School Certificate achieving 7 Credits, which, as far as I was concerned, was excellent. I turned 19 that December and wanted to leave school and get a job. My brother, Osmond, who worked in the Insurance business, knew many farmers in and around Salisbury. We discussed the possibility of my working as an

Assistant on a Tobacco Farm. There was a real possibility of one of the most successful farmers in Mashonaland employing me. Instead, I decided to get my Matric, which would enable me to go to University if I ever wanted to. It would only allow me to go to a South African University, as the University of Rhodesia in Salisbury required 'A' levels. I could not stay at school for another two years.

As it turned out, my final year at school went very quickly. Sadly, I failed to 'Matriculate!' I achieved good marks (for me) in English Literature and History, but failed Mathematics. Somewhere along the line, I must have lost the plot in Math, as when I was younger, I had achieved good marks in Math.

As we were all about to leave school, my classmates and I were concerned about what we would do with our lives. I remember one discussion where I had forcibly declared that I would not join the Railways or the Civil Service whatever I did. I may have said it, but it appeared that God had other ideas. We will look at that a little further on in my story.

THE OVERLAND SAFARI

We lived in Salisbury, and my sister, Avril, worked in Bulawayo and boarded with the Van Rensburg's. Before going to University, my eldest brother's girlfriend was Mavis van Rensburg, a lovely girl. Avril worked for the Rhodesia Railways in their typing pool, but at the end of May in 1963, she and a friend worked their notice before leaving to go and work in England. One morning, shortly after commencing their one-month notice, she read an exciting announcement in the Bulawayo Chronicle. An Overland Safari group was looking for two young women to join their overland trip to England with another female member.

With great excitement, my sister showed the advertisement to her friend. They decided it was for them, and as the Safari was leaving within a week, they had to move very quickly. When the women explained the situation, the company allowed them to leave early, paying them what was owing, and they were off on the adventure of a lifetime.

My mother, Uncle Fred and my brothers were not at all impressed. I was the only one that supported her, possibly, because I was not fully aware of the dangers that she may encounter along the way. Had I known the dangers that she would encounter, I am sure that I, too, would have cautioned her against going! Nevertheless, she went, and by God's grace, she had the adventure of a lifetime and survived to tell the tale. On her journey, she wrote long letters home and recently wrote a book called, about her journey using those same letters. Her book is titled, "Overland Safari -From Rhodesia to England- June to September 1963." By Avril Dunley-Owen.

It is truly an amazing story, but as I have already said, I would have been totally against her going on this journey had I known what I know now. However, that is her story and not mine.

MY HOLIDAY IN NORTHERN RHODESIA

During the 1963/64 six-week Christmas holidays, Osmond arranged a holiday for me with a former Plumtree school friend in Northern Rhodesia. His friend had moved up north and was now farming in the Mkushi farming block some miles to the north of the capital, Lusaka. I had previously visited Lusaka a couple of times with my mother to visit her cousin and family but had never been as far north as the Mkushi farming block.

As my brother's friend, Terry Payne, was in Salisbury, he was able to take me back with him. We drove through Southern Rhodesia, over the Zambezi River Bridge into Northern Rhodesia to Lusaka, and on to Kapiri Mposhi along the Great North Road till we turned off to the farm. The Mkushi Farming Block was an affluent area of farmland that the Northern Rhodesian government had opened up to Commercial farmers, which in those days would have been mostly 'European' farmers from Southern Rhodesia. They told me that the top soil was several feet thick, whereas, in Southern Rhodesia, it was only inches thick.

Terry's application for one of the farms, and he had only moved onto the farm a short while before. The land was well forested, but the government had cleared a large area using huge machinery to rip out the trees by the roots. The farmer was responsible for removing the fallen trees, preparing the land and planting his crops. When I arrived, the preparation of the land had yet to begin. The trees still had to be chopped up and the ground prepared, but Terry had already accomplished a tremendous amount. I arrived late at night to discover the partially completed house where Terry lived. There was no electricity and he used 'Tilley' lamps to light the house. Despite it being primitive, it was great fun.

I thoroughly enjoyed my holiday on the farm and got to know quite a few people while there. One chap about the same age as me and who went to school in Salisbury had to get back for a dental appointment before starting the new term. We arranged to hitch hike together, as no one was travelling to Salisbury when we needed to leave. On the appointed day, Terry dropped us off at Kapiri Mposhi, a small town on the Great North Road, and so began an unforgettable journey.

There was the usual number of cars on the road that day, but it was hours before a car stopped and gave us a lift. We eventually arrived at Chirundu and went down to the border on the Zambezi River banks. After hours of fruitless waiting, we visited the local hotel, where we asked if, in the event of us failing to get a lift by nightfall, we could doss on a couch for the night. The proprietor agreed, and we went out once more to see if we could get a lift. It was already dusk when we decided to try one last car. The car approached with its lights already on, slowed down, and praise God; we had a lift.

As two white boys, we were a little apprehensive upon discovering that our benefactors were black men. However, we hopped in, and off we went across the bridge and into Southern Rhodesia. We had no sooner left the border town's lights when the driver turned off his lights, and we travelled by moonlight. He explained that his alternator had gone, and he was driving on his battery. As we drove along the road, I was amazed to see a large Elephant on the side of the road; it was a good thing he never decided to cross, as we would not have seen him until it was too late.

After some time, we arrived at Makuti, and our driver said that he would not continue until daylight as it was too dangerous to travel any further, and he did not want to be stopped by the police. We thanked our new friends and advised them that we would try to get another lift, as my friend had an appointment in Salisbury in the morning. We hoped that our next ride would be in a car with no problems involving the alternator or battery, enabling us to travel with working lights!

It was freezing at Makuti that night, and other travellers like us had started small fires on the side of the road to warm themselves. We did the same thing and took every stick we could find in the moonlight and made a small fire. Despite the fire and putting on almost every bit of clothing we had, we were still cold. Every time we saw the headlights, we rose to our feet and tried to thumb a lift. At last, after what seemed like several hours, a car stopped, and we had a lift.

The car's occupants were coloureds or people from a mixed heritage, and at that time of the night, in the dim light of the moon, they seemed like a pretty rough lot. However, we were grateful for a lift and climbed aboard. When we got to Karoi, another town on our journey, they left the main road and went to drop off something, or someone, before we continued. They finally dropped us off in Sinoia, where we once again stood at the side of the road.

A big truck stopped some hours later, and another black driver offered us a ride in the cab. He took us to Salisbury, where he dropped me near my home around 7 miles out of town at about 5.00 am. He dropped my friend off near the city centre with plenty of time to get to his dental appointment. It was a long tiring journey, in fact over 400 miles, and it had taken us the best part of 24 hours, but, Praise God; He had been watching over us, I am sure!

CHURCH

Once I had my bicycle, I decided to locate a church, so one day, my friend Helge and I set out to visit the nearest Anglican Church, which happened to be in Mabelreign, where I went to school. It took us some time to find the church as it was quite a distance from my home. We attended the evening service, but I never went back, as it seemed too far to ride every Sunday to make it a regular thing. Nevertheless, distance did not stop me from earning money, as you will discover as you read the next story.

THE NEWSPAPER ROUND

One day a neighbour of ours came around and asked if he could have a word with our servant. He wanted to know whether California would be interested in delivering the Sunday Newspaper to earn a little extra money. It seemed that whoever had been doing it was no longer available.

Although California was not well-educated, he was not stupid. He knew all about the big dogs that patrolled our neighbours' properties, so he turned down the opportunity to earn a little extra money as he was not interested in risking his life. I do not know whether I volunteered or whether our neighbour asked me, but I ended up as possibly the only 'European' Newspaper boy in Rhodesia.

Our neighbour suggested that I ride into town and buy my Sunday newspapers from the first newspaper seller I came across. I would pay the full price and then charge significantly more to deliver them to our neighbours, and depending on how many customers I was able to sign up, I could potentially make a fair amount of cash. Nevertheless, I would need to visit the neighbours first to find out how many were willing to pay the extra price to have their Sunday newspaper delivered to their door.

Most people were happy to pay the price that I would be charging, as it would cost them a lot more to go and collect the newspapers themselves. However, the dogs that California was afraid of were a real problem. Once, I arrived at one home and was pleased to discover that the dog was fast asleep. He was a huge dog and woke up when I knocked on the door. His reaction was terrifying, giving me the distinct impression that he intended to have me for afternoon tea. I waited in vain to be rescued by the householder, but no one was at home, and all I had to defend myself was my hat. I finally made it off the veranda, and to my bike, in one piece. I decided that they would not be receiving newspapers on my rounds, no matter how much they offered.

Despite the dogs, I enjoyed my newspaper round as each Sunday I made around $1.00 in profit. There was one home that was a real problem. I never managed to ride past and always ended up pushing my bike past that house. No matter how quietly I went past this fenceless and gateless property, the little dog would spot me. He would make such a racket that a huge dog would awaken and come running down the drive to stop me in my tracks. I would hold my bike in front of me and await his pleasure before proceeding. Every week I made up my mind that he would not stop me, and every week I would lose my nerve and have to push my bike past the property.

HAVE BIKE WILL DELIVER NEWSPAPERS!

I do not know how far I rode every Sunday morning on my newspaper round, but it would have been a good deal further than I would have cycled had I gone to church. It seemed as if I was undoubtedly drifting away from the Lord.

However, He would not let me go and was about to step into my life once again. How it happened involves two letters in particular.

LIFE CHANGING LETTERS

A) THE LETTER FROM CAPE TOWN

You may remember Margaret Pratt, my neighbour in Cape Town? Well, I was quite taken with Margaret and started corresponding with her after returning to Rhodesia. I found it difficult to read her replies because she would tell me all about her current boyfriend, which was not something that I wished to read. However, I continued to write letters in reply, despite the current boyfriends.

One day I received a letter from Margaret that was very different. It made such an impression on my life that I retained this letter for many years until it sadly disappeared. In this particular letter, she told me about the latest 'man in her life' whose name was Jesus the Saviour of mankind. She told me about her dramatic conversion and how she and her parents attended a lively church in Claremont. She not only spoke about her conversion, but she asked me where I stood with God? One of the Scriptures that she quoted was so powerful that I have never forgotten it, as it challenged my cold-hearted response to the Lord at that time.

"I know thy works, that thou art neither cold nor hot; I would that thou wert cold or hot. So then, because thou art lukewarm, and neither cold nor hot, I will spue thee out of My mouth."
Revelation 3:15-16 KJV

When I had attended the 'Youth for Christ' meeting with Margaret and her friends, no one had responded to the Gospel except myself. I had drifted away, but now, Margaret had got well and truly saved, and the words that she quoted from the Scriptures convicted me deeply! Praise God, He had not forgotten me, and He was still working in my life.

B) LETTERS TO AND FROM THE ARMY

As I was about to leave school and start work, I was concerned about my obligation to do my National service. Wanting to get it over with before I started work, I decided to contact the Army and request a call-up as soon as I finished school. It made sense to me to get my 4 ½ months military service commitment out of the way. After discussing it with my mother and Uncle Fred, I sent off the letter and was given a call-up date at the beginning of January 1965.

After that, my parents decided to go to Cape Town on holiday in January 1965, and Uncle Fred asked if I would like to accompany them. I replied that I sure would, but I had already received my call-up papers from the army. He suggested that I write to the military and explain the situation and ask for a later date. My reply was that we are talking about 'The Army', and there was no way that they would respond positively. However, God was at work, and after writing to the army, they responded by sending me call-up papers for February 1965 instead. As I have already said, God was at work!

THE HOLIDAY JOB

Although I was making the 'grand total' of around $1.00 every Sunday, that was not a great deal of money for a holiday in Cape Town, so I was pleased when Uncle Fred offered me a temporary job where he worked. He was Works Manager and had spoken to the General

Manager who had agreed to employ me in an interim capacity. It was a 'dog's body' type of job helping out in several situations, mainly filing documents. Nevertheless, it was a job!

When I arrived at work on my first day, Uncle Fred asked me what wage I expected for my labours. I had no idea and told him so. He said that I ought to know what I was worth when I apply for a job, which is good advice, but for someone happy to receive $1.00 every Sunday delivering newspapers, it was difficult to answer. Nevertheless, I was thrilled to be given $1.00 a day, and after two months, I had enough for my holiday. I enjoyed my time working at British Cellophane in Salisbury. It was good work experience for me to have before starting work in earnest.

Chapter 4

THE HOLIDAY IN CAPE TOWN

After a three-day journey by car of around 1,500 miles, we arrived in Cape Town, just after lunch, early in January 1965. Because we had arrived earlier than anticipated, we needed to find something to do before presenting ourselves at the home of our hosts. We had arranged to stay with the Harbour Master, Joe Armstrong, who had previously arranged my trip up the coast to Walvis Bay a couple of years before, and his wife, Margaret.

After some discussion, we decided to visit the Pratt's, who had been our next-door neighbours when we lived in Cape Town. I think it was a Saturday and Margaret, the girl next door, had her latest boyfriend visiting. They welcomed us warmly, and while my parents spent time with the older folk, I joined the younger people somewhere else in the house. I soon discovered that they were both on 'fire' for the Lord, and they lost no time in asking me where I stood with God.

Although a few years before I had had a real encounter with the Lord, sadly by this stage, I was so far off track that when they asked if I believed that I was going to heaven, I replied, "I hope so! I am sure that when my deeds are weighed in the balance that my good deeds will outweigh my bad deeds."

Anyhow, not wanting to be out-maneuvered, I then went on the attack and said, "Well, what about you? Do you think that you are going to heaven?"

They were confident about going to heaven when

they died! They took time to explain that it was not because of what they had done; it was because they believed in the Lord Jesus Christ! We spent a long time discussing spiritual things before they asked me whether I would like to accompany them to see a film show that night. I was only too happy to accept, after all, I was on holiday. However, it is also possible that I was under the impression that we were going to 'the movies!'

After speaking to all involved, we agreed that I would spend the night at our former neighbour's home, and sometime the next day, they would take me out to Hout Bay.

That night we never went to 'the movies', but I saw a fantastic Christian film at the local Assembly of God church that changed my life. The film was the true story about a famous singer whose parents ran a mission on 'Skid Row' in Los Angeles in the USA. He and his beautiful wife were unbelievers and living 'The High Life.' They despised his parents' work. One day, tragedy struck, and he was critically injured in a motor accident. In desperation, with her husband unlikely to live, his wife asked a Christian preacher to pray for her husband's healing. When he was miraculously healed, she became a believer in the Lord Jesus Christ. Instead of being grateful, the singer was furious when he learned that she had called in a preacher of the Gospel to pray for him. His anger continued when he later discovered that although he would live, he would never sing again.

The story continued and had a happy ending when he accepted Jesus as his Saviour and committed his life and talents to The King's service. God restored his voice, and although he was given a hard time by the record company that had previously recorded his songs, from then on, he sang only the praises of The Lord.

As I watched the story unfold that night, I realised that in some way, I identified with the singer and needed to get right with God, so by the end of the evening, I was wonderfully restored to my Lord. From then on, if anyone asks me the question that I had my friends had asked that afternoon, I can say with confidence that if I die, I know that I would go home to be with Jesus in Heaven.

I stayed overnight with the Pratt's and attended the Sunday morning service with them at the Claremont Assembly of God, where I had been the night before. I soon discovered that it was a very lively church, and for the first time in my life, I heard the gifts of the Holy Spirit in operation. I also had the privilege of sitting under the Holy Spirit anointed ministry of Paul Lange, one of the most anointed preachers I have ever heard.

I was so pleased to be there that I made sure that I did not miss a meeting for the next three weeks of my holiday. Some years before, I had failed to respond enthusiastically after the 'Youth for Christ' meeting, but I would not make the same mistake twice. Attending these twice-weekly meetings meant catching the last bus at night, from Wynberg (near Claremont) to Hout Bay, a small coastal town. However, during that short holiday, I was saved, baptised by full immersion in water, and had a mighty Holy Spirit anointing before returning to Rhodesia.

Arriving in Hout Bay late at night, instead of climbing the hill to the house where we were staying, I decided to go for a walk on the beach in the moonlight as I had a few things to sort out before going to sleep. I remember walking along the beach at the water's edge with the wind blowing the sand and the surf. Although I was sure of my salvation, I had a battle going on, so as I walked the beach, I recited a few of the verses that I had learned.

"Believe on the Lord Jesus Christ, and you will be saved, ---." Acts 16.31

"--- whoever calls on the name of the Lord shall be saved." Acts 2.21

"Behold, I stand at the door and knock. If anyone hears My voice and opens the door, I will come in to him and dine with him and he with Me." Revelation3.20

As I repeated these verses slowly, the assurance of my salvation calmed my spirit, and I was able to leave the beach, climb the hill and go to sleep. I took the path up the hill, which was a lot shorter than going along the road. However, it was late at night, and the trail led through a lot of overhanging shrubbery and trees, so it was a relief to finally arrive at my destination.

Fortunately, I was sleeping on the verandah, so my arrival did not disturb the family. Our host left for work very early in the mornings.

One night while saying my prayers, I became very conscious of God's presence, and He just seemed to clothe me with His Spirit. It was a wonderful experience that I have never forgotten.

During my visit to the Assembly in Cape Town, Paul Lange spoke on Baptism, The Baptism of the Holy Spirit, The Rapture, the Resurrection of the Dead, the Second Coming, and Eternal Judgement. I took notes at each service, which I went through when I arrived home. I was amazed at what I had learned in such a short time, and now I took my Bible everywhere.

One evening we travelled into Claremont from Hout Bay so that my parents could visit some friends while I went to the Bible Study. As we were early for our visit, Uncle Fred decided to have a drink, so we stopped off at a hotel for a sundowner. In those days, I enjoyed a beer. After our sundowner, they dropped me off at the Pratt's so that I could get a lift to the Bible Study with the family. When I arrived, the first thing that Margaret said was, "Oh, you've been drinking!"

I replied very forcibly, "No, I have not been drinking. I have had a beer on the way here, but I have not been drinking!"

Nevertheless, what she said got me thinking, and a few days later, I made a life-changing decision.
The Lord impressed upon my spirit that I needed to give up drinking alcohol altogether one day as we enjoyed the drive around the Cape Peninsula, a most spectacular marine drive known as Chapman's Peak Drive. I leaned forward in the car and said to my mother and Uncle Fred that I would not drink alcohol from that day on.

They were well aware that something was happening in my life but accepted my decision with a little bit of humour as they did not expect it to last. In his younger days, my stepfather had been a Jehovah's Witness for a short while but had fallen away, and so I think he expected my decision to follow Christ to be only for a short time. For a long time afterward, if I were at home, he would always pour me a drink along with one for my mother and himself. That may have been because he liked to have an extra sherry, or it may have been that he never really expected my decision to last. However, I believed that God spoke to me, and from that day to this, I have been a 'teetotaller'.

It could not have been long after this, as I was only in Cape Town for three weeks when my new friends asked if I wanted to be baptised in water. Naturally, I said that I would love to be baptised, as I was keen to receive whatever God had for me, and I was completely open to God's Word. They approached the minister on my behalf, and he agreed to arrange a special meeting to baptise me before we returned home.

However, a few days before that great day arrived, we visited some of my late dad's long-lost relatives. They had a son about my age, and it was a joy to discover that he was a believer and planning to become a Baptist Minister. I told him all about my recent experiences, which I am sure thrilled him. He then asked me what I knew about the Assemblies of God, the church I was attending? I explained that I had not even heard of a church called the Assemblies of God until I had arrived in Cape Town a few days before.

My cousin was concerned about me and suggested that we see his minister for a chat, which I was only too happy to do. The Baptist Minister suggested that I postpone my baptism until I returned to Rhodesia and became established in a local church. I was pleased to receive this advice as it seemed the wisest thing to do, so I planned to call off my baptism until a later date. However, God knew what He was doing, and He had a different plan.

Because the Baptismal Service had been specially arranged for me, and the day was fast approaching, I needed to tell Paul Lange, the minister, as soon as possible. He had to know that if there were to be baptism service, it would have to proceed without me!

Several things happened which caused me to miss my lift to the midweek Bible Study, and I arrived late. Desperate to get to the meeting for more than one reason, I borrowed a bicycle from one of my old friends and finally made it to church just after the service had begun.

When I finally arrived, I could not get into the building as it was so packed, so I had to listen from outside the window. It was not long after this that the congregation moved into a new 300 seat building known as the Harfield Road Assembly. A few years later, it was again so full that two new congregations started with 100 people going off in one direction and 150 in another.

However, to get back to my story, just before Paul Lange gave the Bible study, he gave some announcements, including the fact that there would be a baptismal service in my honour. Unbeknown to him, I was looking through the window and had something to say about that, as I had changed my mind.

As usual, it was a great meeting. Paul was a fantastic teacher of God's Word. I can still remember many of his messages, which I heard at least 40-50 years ago. Still, I was on a mission, and as soon as I could speak to him, I told him of my decision to postpone being baptised in water. Paul, a very big man, looked down at me and gently went through the record of the baptisms recorded in the book of Acts and asked me how long people waited before being baptised.

We, first of all, looked at the converts on the day of Pentecost, who I had to agree had been baptised on the very same day they were converted! We then looked at those who were saved in the house of Cornelius, the Roman Centurion, and once again, I had to agree that it was clear that they too were baptised, most likely the same day. As we went through the Scriptures, it became clear that all new converts were baptised just as soon as they could be after they asked the Lord Jesus to save them. I had no choice but to reply that they did not wait. He then laid his hand on my head and prayed, and I felt the anointing of the Holy Spirit and realised that I had to be baptised as planned and not put it off, as God was leading me that way.

At my baptism, someone gave me a Bible Verse, possibly Mrs. Pratt, that has been a great encouragement to me over the years. The verse was,

" … being confident of this very thing, that He who has begun a good work in you will complete it until the day of Jesus Christ; …" Philippians 1.6

Unfortunately, when the great day arrived, my parents did not witness my baptism because when I decided to postpone my baptism until I returned to Rhodesia, they made plans to visit some other friends. Because our time in Cape Town was so limited, they did not want to cancel their visit. The only friend, not part of the church family, who witnessed my baptism was Vivian, the girl whose party I had attended some years before. Although her brother got saved some years later, she had still not trusted in Jesus as her Saviour the last time I saw her.

Having now been baptised in water, my friends in Cape Town asked me whether they could pray for me to be baptised in the Holy Spirit? I was delighted for them to pray for me to be filled with the Holy Spirit before I left for home because I had witnessed the exercising of the Holy Spirit's vocal gifts, and I heard and believed the outstanding teaching given by Paul Lange since my first visit to that church.

As time was short and I was leaving within a couple of days, we decided to meet on the Sunday afternoon between the services to pray, and those who were there prayed for me. They laid hands upon me and prayed that the Lord would fill me with His Spirit. As we were praying and seeking God, the power of the Lord overshadowed me, and I did not doubt the presence of God. I had my head down, not an ideal posture to receive the Holy Spirit, and I had my hands and my fingers locked together. The presence of God was so powerful that I could not get my hands apart. They seemed welded together. I felt that I might never be able to get my hands apart again!

Eventually, I was able to get my hands open, but instead of letting God finish with me, all I could think of was going to see my friends who still lived across the road from where we used to live and telling them about the Lord. As soon as I could, I went to see them and told them what had been happening to me. I had seen them several times while in Cape Town, and I am sure it was one of their bicycles that I borrowed when I planned to cancel my baptism, the day that I nearly missed the Bible Study.

I was a little hasty that day and should have waited until God had finished with me. However, He is faithful, and although it would be some years before I would 'speak in tongues' and have the assurance that I had received all that God had for me, I knew that He was with me and would never forsake me.

All too soon, it was time to say goodbye and return home, but my holiday had been genuinely memorable. So much had taken place in such a short time. I was honestly a new man, restored to the Lord, baptised in water, and experienced such a mighty touch from God. Praise His wonderful name. It was now time to go back home to Rhodesia.

I remember two incidents clearly on the long journey back home, about 1,500 miles.

THE JOURNEY HOME

My mother arranged to spend a night or two with some friends in Johannesburg on the way home. Our hosts were the mother of one of my brother's friends and her new husband. While visiting, I had the opportunity of explaining to them all about my recent experiences of getting right with God. Our host revealed that he was also a firm believer, not in the Lord Jesus Christ, but in UFO's and Extra-Terrestrial beings, which fascinated me. I had only just learned about the soon-coming 'rapture' of believers when Jesus comes for His 'Bride' the Church. When we discussed 'The Rapture', I also learned that when it occurs, the nations' leaders will have a hard time explaining away this event to the people left behind. Nevertheless, one of the possibilities will be that they will say that the Christians were taken away by extraterrestrial beings! The people left will believe anything, but what the Bible has to say about this fantastic event!

We were soon on our way again, and while in the Northern Transvaal, we came upon a terrible accident. It happened just a mile or two in front of us, on a straight section of the road. Uncle Fred, who was driving, witnessed the entire event. An oncoming car strayed onto the right-hand side of the road, directly in the path of another vehicle. He saw them have a head-on collision. My mother and I had not seen the crash, but we did see the consequences a few minutes later. It was terrible to see several bodies strewn across the road as we arrived on the scene.

As soon as others arrived, some with medical training, we went to the nearest farmhouse to use the telephone to call for help, as this was, of course, long before mobile phones. However, before we went to the farmhouse, I handed over a much-loved metal water bottle to one of the helpers to give water to whoever needed it. Sadly, I never saw it again, as when we arrived back from the farmhouse, there were plenty of helpers on the scene, and so we were soon on our way, much sobered by what we had just seen.

Being the only eyewitness of the accident, Uncle Fred had to attend a South African court case.

Chapter 5

MILITARY SERVICE

HOME

We arrived home only a few days before I was due to go into the army. Naturally, there was a lot to do before leaving for Llewellyn Barracks, just outside Bulawayo. My friend, Helge, came around for a visit, and I shared the good news of my salvation with him. It would be some years before he responded to the Gospel and only once he moved to South Africa.

Helge had found employment in the retail trade with a particularly hard-headed businessman. He earned very little and worked long hours, but he learned the trade, which stood him in good stead for the future. He purchased an electric bicycle with his meager resources, which took him everywhere, rather slowly, but very economically, which was the most important thing for him. He was a good friend, and I am sorry that we lost contact many years ago.

We visited Jimmy and Doris Clerk during the weekend, some relatives who had a lovely house in Bulawayo. I am sure that Doris's brother-in-law, my Uncle Charles, had built the house for them. It boasted a swimming pool and a tennis court, and many years later, Craig and Georgie Friend bought it. When we were visiting from the UK, Mally and I stayed some nights with them, in my uncle's old house.

Uncle Jimmy had been a member of the Federal Government, and on that day, my late dad's brother,

Uncle Cyril, was also visiting. When he heard that I was travelling to Llewellyn on the overnight train the next day, he asked whether I had a job lined up after I came out of the army. Sadly, I have never been ahead of the game, so I had not even tried to find employment. However, let me be clear, as I have mentioned elsewhere, I had decided not to join the Railways or the Civil Service.

All the same, like it or not, God was at work, and as he was Regional Manager of the Eastern Region of The Railways, Uncle Cyril asked whether I had considered The Railways? I replied, truthfully, that I had not considered the Railways. That Sunday night, he was travelling in a private coach on the same train as me, and he suggested that if I write a letter applying for work and give it to him at the station; he would see that it was delivered to the personnel department in Bulawayo the following day. He also told me that they would most likely contact me for an interview while I was in the Army, and providing all went well, I would have a job to go to when I came out of the army.

Reluctantly, I drafted a letter and handed it to my uncle at the station the following night. Sometime later, I received some forms, which I filled in, and later still attended an interview in Bulawayo. As a result, when I left The Army, I became a Rhodesia Railways employee like many of my relatives before me. No matter what I had said previously, I know that God had gone before me!

THE ROYAL RHODESIAN REGIMENT, LLEWELLYN BARRACKS, HEANY JUNCTION.

My friends in Cape Town had given me some excellent advice for my return home when they realised that I would be doing my National Service. They advised me very strongly to make my position clear from the very first day. They said that if I did not confess Christ the first day, it would be harder to do each following day. Travelling to Llewellyn Barracks on the top bunk in my train compartment, I knelt and prayed before going to sleep. That was easy; I had begun; however, no one could see!

The next day we received our kit, and in true army style, we were shouted at by all and sundry. They advised us that there would be an inspection the following morning and we better be ready for it. Some of the men in the barrack-room stayed up all night to make sure everything was shiny and clean. Inspection or not, I needed my sleep, so when I thought that I had done enough, I prepared to go to bed. It was crunch time. Getting down on my knees and praying in a barrack room of around 30 men was quite daunting. However, down on my knees, I went, but that night I confess, I prayed little, half expecting a boot to come my way. However, once I had prayed, I got in or on to my bed and went to sleep.

The interesting thing about my prayer on that first night was that a more mature Christian believer, in another barrack-room, came to hear about it, and within a matter of days, came looking for me. He was a real loud Pentecostal and was quite an embarrassment to me at times. Remember, I was more used to the Anglican

Church at that stage of my life and had only had exposure to Pentecost for around three weeks.

My new friend proved to be a real blessing, and the two of us used to meet up together for prayer. As time went by, our numbers increased as other born-again believers came to join us. I thank God for this brother in Christ who was such a blessing to me, although I did not always appreciate him at the time.

I cannot say that I enjoyed my time at Llewellyn, but the initial six-week training went very quickly. I had never been in better shape physically in all my life. We ate a lot, but the amount of marching, running and exercise kept us fit. At mealtimes, we all took anything up to six slices of bread to supplement our meal; however, that was not to continue. The Army's catering department concluded that we were eating far too much bread, so they limited the amount of bread that we were allowed giving us old army ration biscuits instead. I think they must have been surplus from the Second World War as they were not fresh by any means.

Towards the end of our initial six weeks of training, we had a weekend pass, and I travelled home to Salisbury. We had to be back by midnight on Sunday, but as I wanted to enjoy as much time at home as possible, I managed to arrange a lift back to the barracks on Sunday afternoon. Not long after we left Salisbury on our 280-mile journey to Bulawayo, I realised that all my companions had been drinking, including the driver! The drive back to barracks turned out to be a 'pub crawl'. We stopped at the Half Way Hotel at Selous, then in Hartley, Gatooma, Que Que, and Gwelo. Due to the amount of alcohol they had consumed, I became quite alarmed, as my companions were worse for wear, and I was the only sober man in the car who was by now known as 'Pepsi'.

I seriously considered leaving my friends at Gwelo, but as we still had 100 miles to go, and to hitch a lift at night was never easy (as I had previously experienced), I stayed with the car. I offered to drive, but the driver refused, so we set off once again on the last leg of the journey with me 'praying without ceasing'. Not far from Gwelo, we very nearly left the road and narrowly avoided a culvert that did help sober up the driver and the others a little. Anyhow, praise God, we eventually arrived, but I think it was only just in time as they had drunk the night away.

Before the end of our initial six weeks of training, we went on an overnight trip to the rifle range. We were all issued with the regular army ration pack for 24 hours and camped out in the open after a day at the range. It is important to mention that I was recognised as a marksman and awarded a badge to sew on to my uniform. I am convinced that the guy next to me must have been firing at my target, making me the marksman.

That night we ended up camping right alongside a farmer's field of ripe mealies, which were a great temptation to our company. We made many fires so that we could roast lovely fresh mealies. Unsurprisingly, the following morning, the Sergeant Major informed, in his usual loud voice, us that the farmer was not impressed to discover that his field had been raided. He had gone down to the field early in the morning and found the discarded leaves of possibly hundreds of mealies, leading right to our camp.

The Sergeant Major reprimanded us, saying that we were a bunch of thieves. He then told us that we were not very good ones at that, as we had led the farmer right to our camp by discarding the leaves from the farmer's field to our campsite. He then commanded all those responsible for taking one step forward and owning up to what they had done. I was shocked and still am when not one member of the company owned up. Over the years, when I have thought about that incident, I have concluded that I ought to have taken one step back, as I am reasonably sure that I was one of the only ones not to have eaten a mealie the night before!

When not one member of the company owned up to the offense, we were all put on a charge and informed that the penalty would involve Jankers and a fine. Jankers involved repeatedly reporting to the Guard House, where they would inspect your uniform, drill you and send you back to your barracks to change into another uniform. The process would be repeated time and again. As a result, I was not at all happy to have to pay for a crime that I had not committed. However, God was good, as I never had to pay up or do Jankers as I moved to Brady Barracks before the punishment took place.

BRADY BARRACKS

As we came to the end of our six weeks initial training, they gave us a choice to remain with the riflemen move to another corps such as Signals, Engineers, or the Medics. I had just committed to Christ before entering The Army, and therefore, really did not want to kill anyone, so I chose to move. Yet, when my brothers had done their military service, I could remember them speaking of the Medics as 'spastics'. My best bet was to become a medic whose job was to save lives, but I did not want my brothers thinking of me as a 'spastic', so I had a dilemma. After a lot of thought and I hope prayer, I opted to join the Signals, who, although armed, were responsible for communications rather than fighting. I was accepted and was able to say goodbye to Llewellyn Barracks and move on to Brady Barracks.

During initial training, all you are required to do is follow orders giving your mind a rest as you are not encouraged to think for yourself. Your primary responsibility is to follow orders. However, when you are training to be an army signaller, you have to start thinking again as you have to learn things like Morse Code, Radio-signalling, Aerials, and a host of other things. As my brain had been largely inactive for six weeks, it took me a couple of weeks to start thinking again. Despite my brain beginning to function normally again, my training as an army signaller was not particularly successful. On one occasion, the instructor called me a 'dozy dodo', which was insulting as we all know the dodo is extinct. Besides, when Ian Smith, our Prime Minister, offered Rhodesian Troops to assist the USA in Vietnam, someone, somewhere, suggested that if they include me, I would be more helpful to the Americans if they sent me to the Viet Cong! However, I have a 'thick skin',and I could take it!

At Brady, there were a few 'regular' Army personnel training with us. In our Barracks, There was a hard man always picking on someone or looking for a fight. When I felt he had gone far enough with one guy, I told him to stop. He immediately asked what I would do if he didn't, and I could see that he was looking for a fight. However, he did not know what I was made of and, Praise God, he never found out. I was able to stop his bullying and keep him guessing for the remainder of my time at Brady.

When we moved into our new barracks, we quickly discovered we had to go through an initiation. As a result, we were marched up to the canteen, while unbeknown to us, knowing full well that there was an inspection in the morning, others messed up our barrack room. Having arrived at the canteen, we were instructed to down two beers at the double. However, less than two months before, I had given up alcohol for good, and so I had to say, "Sorry, I do not drink."

The response was something like this, "Too bad. Tonight, you will drink two beers."

To which I replied, "No, I do not drink."

Eventually, because I was so insistent and was not going to back down, they told me that I could skip the beers but instead, I must drink three Cokes at the double! Now I do not know about you, but that is an impossibility. Have you ever drunk one Coke at the double, let alone three? I have no idea how far I got, but eventually, we returned to our Barracks and were told that they were a disgrace and that we had better get them ready for the inspection the next morning. Before we went to the canteen, it looked great, but 'they' had messed it up. Who 'they' were, we never did find out. When you are new, you follow orders no matter who is giving them, provided they shout loud enough!

Sometime after this, I watched a film on television in the canteen, and when it finished, I had to walk past some guys who had been drinking quite heavily. By this time, everyone knew that I did not drink; however, one chap who was a friend of mine would always invite me to have a drink. He would say that one drink will not hurt you and so on. As was his habit, he called out to me and invited me to have a drink. I replied as always that I did not drink. Be that as it may, the regular army guy was there, and he opened a beer (the Canteen was already closed, but a few full beers and a large number of empties were on the table) and handed it to me. I politely said, "No thanks," as I do not drink.

He did not like me refusing his hospitality and took an empty bottle and broke it over the back of a chair and held it up to my face, and said, "Drink it!"

I insisted, "No, as I have already said, I do not drink!"

By this time, the guy who had called me over had sobered up a little, and when he saw what was happening, he told me to beat it while he calmed the other guy down, which I did. However, I was very grateful to God for looking after me that night and every night.

One of the men in the barrack room was a believer, and one Sunday, when we had a pass, he invited me to church and then home for lunch at his parents' home. The church he and his family attended was very different from anything that I had thus far come across. For one thing, they sang hymns without musical accompaniment and were very quiet. For them, Sunday was the Lord's day, and therefore they did not read the Sunday papers, listen to the radio or TV, or participate in sport or anything else that would take away from the spiritual reason for the day. They were lovely people and a real blessing to me, although their experience was very different.

One last thing about my time at Brady involves a

very foolish exercise. One night shortly before we were due to finish our training, one of the guys came up with a plan to go out to the Drive-In Cinema to watch a film. He had noticed that the Officers wore similar headgear to the RLI (Rhodesian Light Infantry), the unit to which our aggressive Regular Army belonged. That night he borrowed a peaked cap and drove out of the gate pretending to be an officer, and we went to the Drive-In Cinema with him. Another chap and I hid in the back of the car. Why I did it, I have no idea. If we had been caught we would have spent a lot longer in the army than we had planned, and it would have been in the guardhouse. We can only thank God that the guard was asleep that night (not literally), as we would not have got away with it. However, things were changing in Rhodesia, and those on guard duty would need to be more awake as trouble was on the horizon!

CHAPTER 6

A CIVILIAN AGAIN

It was good to come home to Stortford after 4 ½ months away in The Army. We would soon be moving to a lovely house that Uncle Fred had purchased, 'Jabula', which is Zulu for 'Rejoice'. It was opposite the Salisbury Gliding Club, on the road that ran between the Bulawayo road and the Old Gatooma Road. Once again, my bedroom would be an outside room, which we improved in time to include a toilet and shower.

I had the best of both worlds. I had all the independence that I could ask for and a loving mother who even brought me a cup of tea in bed every morning. If I arrived home late, my food was in the plate oven, and if I were very late, it would be a little dry and burnt. However, I usually had good food and a loving home. We always had dogs, which I took out for walks in the bush. I had an old record player which Osmond had given me. He had purchased it when we lived in Bulawayo, and I had several long-playing records to listen to, so life was great.

Coming and going as and when I chose was not possible without transport. There was no suitable public transport from where we lived on the Old Gatooma Road at Stortford, in Tynwald. Initially, I got a lift with Uncle Fred; however, it was not easy. I finished work at 4.30 pm near the City Centre, and he finished at 5.30 pm or later in the Industrial Centre some way away, so there was no other option I needed to get some wheels. Yet, as I had only just started work and was under 21 years of age, I could not take out an H.P. (hire purchase) agreement on my own. The salesman advised me that I needed someone to sign as a guarantor before I would be able to proceed. Uncle Fred signed as a guarantor for me to purchase a motorcycle on credit, although he was reluctant to do so. I bought a Honda 150cc Motorcycle, which cost me all of £180.00. It was my pride and joy, and with a black and gold helmet, artificial leather jacket and gloves to match, I was made! I made an impressive sight travelling back and forth to work, particularly when travelling up and down the strip road near where we lived. I may not have shown him real appreciation at the time, but I am truly grateful for his help.

PREPARATION

Chapter 1

A FALSE START

MY NEW MOTORCYCLE

MY HONDA 150CC

THE MAN AND DINGAAN, HIS DOG

When I first started work, I worked in an office in Merchant House, located on Forbes Avenue, just up from the Railway Station in Salisbury, about seven miles from where we lived. The church which was soon to become my 'spiritual home' was McCleary Avenue Assembly of God in Eastlea, on the opposite side of town, which was also around seven miles from where we lived.

Having taken possession of my sparkling new Honda 150cc motorcycle, I travelled to work every morning on my own, instead of relying on an early morning lift, so I arrived at work a lot earlier than was needed. I also no longer had to wait a couple of hours after finishing work for a lift home.

Because the engine on my new bike was so quiet, sometimes while waiting at the 'robots' (for those not from my part of the world, traffic lights), I thought that the engine had stopped. As a result, when the lights turned green, I tried to restart the bike, only to discover that it was still running. I decided to take the baffles out of the exhausts, mainly so that I could hear the engine. However, I must admit that it did sound much more impressive, less like a sewing machine, particularly when I was around my friends who all rode much bigger machines.

MY NEW CHURCH

As a new believer, I knew that it was vital that I got into fellowship and made Christian friends as soon as possible, which proved to be much easier than I expected as there were a lot of young people in the Assembly, and some of them even lived on my side of town. A number of them also rode motorcycles just like me. Well, not quite like me, as my 150cc Honda was by far the smallest bike, as the others all rode much more powerful machines.

Paul and Jonathon Black, brothers who lived with their parents in Mabelreign, rode a Suzuki 300 and Ducati 250cc, respectively. Another guy had an old reconditioned Triumph 500cc. As you can see, my motorcycle was by far the smallest, but that did not stop me from enjoying travelling to and from the meetings, usually some way behind Paul and Jonathan.

One day when Paul was following Jonathan, he was so impressed with how Jonathon took the corner, on the road not far from the Assembly, that he failed to notice that he had arrived at the same corner. As a result, he came off his bike and ended up with a broken arm. Although it is a funny story, it could have been fatal, and the Lord was very gracious in that he only broke his arm.

Another time, as I was travelling into the centre of Salisbury, after the Sunday morning meeting, I was unaware that a policeman was trailing me. As I pulled up at the Central Post Office to check our mailbox (there was no mail delivery where we lived), the policeman pulled up next to me. He gave me a real dressing down and explained that since he had begun following me, which must have been from near the Assembly, I had broken most of the rules of the road. He then went on to tell me all the things that I had done wrong. It was a real wake-up call, but he let me go with 'a caution' despite my transgressions. If it was as bad as he said, I could have lost my license if I had one. I was possibly still a learner at the time. "Praise God, once again, the Lord had been watching over me!"

Sadly, despite being in fellowship and having made some great new Christian friends, all was not well! It was some time that same year that a group of us stopped attending the Assembly and dropped out of fellowship. As I look back on those days, I know that the Lord warned me about what was happening, but I did not know what to do about it at the time.

It happened like this! One night during the rainy season, I arrived at Paul and Jonathan's home, as was my custom, to discover that Paul had borrowed his Dad's car so that we could travel together to the Assembly. After the meeting, we stopped off at the 'Yellow Orchid' Drive-in Restaurant for a coffee on our way home, which was not unusual. It was there that the Lord showed me that something was wrong. Sadly, I didn't say anything about it at the time as I was, after all, the youngest Christian in the car. The others had been believers much longer than I had.

That night the Lord impressed upon my spirit that our conversation was not right. As young single men, surprise, surprise, we talked about girls, motorbikes, work, politics, even our local Assembly, and the people in it. However, sadly, we did not speak about God, neither did we discuss His Word and so on. Although we were all believers, the Lord Jesus was left out of our conversation altogether!

Would to God that I had said something that evening as sadly, within a few weeks, we had all stopped attending the Assembly for one reason or another, and some never went back. Paul, met a girl who was not a believer, and he stopped coming to the Assembly as she was not interested. His brother Jonathan, who was younger than Paul, was possibly influenced by his brother's decision. However, I cannot explain why I allowed myself to drift out of fellowship; I have no explanation. Many years later, I heard that Paul's wife had come to know the Lord as her Saviour. However, Paul had still not made right with God. I hope that he was later restored to fellowship, as he was such a blessing to me as a young Christian.

When discussing what happened to us young men some years later, another young man who had been in the Assembly at that time told me that he had also grown cold to the things of God the year that we all fell away. His name was Rob Day, and he lived almost across the road from the Assembly. He was a precious brother, and his favourite verse at the time was,

"Now, godliness with contentment is great gain." 1 Timothy 6:6

When we discussed it, Rob told me that his heart was backslidden, but he continued to attend the meetings despite that. Instead of dropping out of fellowship, he worked through his problems until he was back in the right relationship with God and His people. Rob had the right idea. There are times when, for one reason or another, we travel through the 'wilderness'. However, that is not the time to quit, as the 'promised land' is just ahead if we will only persevere. As you consider what happened to some of the young men that year, including me, I would ask you to meditate upon the following words from an old song. It goes like this,

"I'd never be a backslider; I'll tell you the reason why I'm afraid that the Lord might call me, and I wouldn't be ready to die."

The songwriter was correct. We cannot afford to stray away from God, the hour is late, and we need to be ready, as Jesus could come at any time. Let us make sure that we take note of the warnings given in Scripture such as,

"Therefore, let him who thinks he stands take heed lest he fall." 1 Corinthians 10:12

Keep close to God, stay in fellowship, study God's Word and talk to Him every day.

Things were about to change significantly in Rhodesia.

THE UNILATERAL DECLARATION OF INDEPENDENCE

As mentioned earlier in this story, Southern Rhodesia, a successful self-governing territory since 1923, joined Northern Rhodesia and Nyasaland, two British colonies, to form the Federation of Rhodesia and Nyasaland in 1953. The Federation was highly successful and brought much-needed development to all three territories. Southern Rhodesia, particularly Salisbury, benefited greatly, as Salisbury was the Capital of Southern Rhodesia and the Federation. As Southern Rhodesia was much more developed than the other two territories, it was able to take full advantage of the situation.

However, 'the winds of change' were blowing a gale through Africa, as mentioned by Harold Macmillan in a speech in Cape Town on the 3rd February 1960. As a result of severe agitation from African Nationalists, the Federation dissolved in 1963 after ten good years. The United Kingdom government granted Nyasaland independence, which became Malawi, on the 6th July 1964. Northern Rhodesia gained independence as Zambia on the 24th of October 1964. However, despite Southern Rhodesia having governed itself successfully since 1923, the British government refused to grant the country full independence until every citizen had the right to vote.

While under the leadership of Prime Ministers Winston Fielding, followed by Ian Smith, The United Kingdom would only grant Southern Rhodesia independence when the government would hold 'one man, one vote' elections. Although that may seem fair to many British citizens, one needs to remember that it took

Britain many years to achieve Universal Suffrage, and the idea of 'one man, one vote' was a very new concept in Africa.

The existing Rhodesian voters looked with horror at what was taking place in other African countries that had adopted this policy. The Rhodesians knew that 'one man, one vote' had come to be understood in Africa as 'one man, one vote, one time', as whoever won the election the first time would never give up power unless forced to do so through a military coup. After many meetings and many suggestions, Ian Smith's government realised that despite the Rhodesian government being willing to make many concessions, the British Government and the African Nationalists were not prepared to back down under any circumstances. Sadly, the African Nationalists or the British Government did not consider the Rhodesians' concessions good enough and rejected them.

And so it was that almost the entire white population, and most likely, a good percentage of the black population, tuned to Rhodesian Broadcasting Corporation at 11.00 am on the 11th day of the 11th Month of 1965. I remember the occasion well because all the staff in my department crowded into one office to listen to the broadcast on a portable radio.

For better or worse, on that day, Ian Douglas Smith, the Prime Minister of the self-governing country of Southern Rhodesia, unilaterally declared independence from Great Britain or UDI as it became known. Everybody was not necessarily in favour of UDI, but all were sympathetic to the country's difficult situation and the Prime Minister at that time.

Possibly not much work took place that day, as

we all considered the future as we knew that things would change dramatically in the coming months. Having witnessed what had happened in other African countries to the north, it appeared to many that if we wanted Rhodesia to continue as a prosperous country for all its inhabitants, our only hope was to cut our ties with the UK and plot our own future, as had been decided by our Prime Minister that morning.

MY TWENTY-FIRST BIRTHDAY

Following that momentous day, almost a month later, we decided to celebrate my 21st Birthday on the 9th of December 1965. We hired a small marquee and erected it on the lawn in preparation for the big day. I invited a beautiful girl to be my date that evening, a member of the British South Africa Police (BSAP). I met her when visiting my cousins. We also invited some relatives, some of my 'backslidden' friends, some old school friends from Ellis Robins, and an old gentleman who was a friend of Uncle Fred. Although I probably received many gifts, I only remember my sister's present, a lovely pair of brown suede shoes. Honestly, I think they were the best shoes that I have ever worn.

It rained all week, heavily soaking the lawn where we planned to erect the marquee. It looked very much as if the party would be a washout. But, amazingly, the day of the party was hot and sunny, the only day it did not rain for around ten days, before and after my party. The wonderful sunshine dried up the lawn before we erected the marquee, and it remained dry the entire evening. My Aunt Dot, who was there that evening and most likely sang *Bless this House*, made the following comment, "Alan, God has been very good to you this evening."

Although I agreed, I could not understand why God would choose to bless me, as I was not living for Him as I should.

As my date lived on the other side of town, I set off early to pick her up, having been given the rare privilege of borrowing the car. The car was a lovely old Rover 90, the pride and joy of Uncle Fred. On my way home from fetching the young lady, I needed to travel to another part of town and pick up my step-father's friend. However, when I arrived at my date's home, she was not there, and no one at her house was aware that she was supposed to be going out with me. I was devastated to find that she was not in, as this was not just any day of the week; this was my 21st birthday party! Had I not been responsible for picking up the elderly gentleman, I think I may have skipped the whole evening, as I was so disappointed. On second thoughts, perhaps not, although that is how I felt!

The elderly man used to play the banjo, and sometime later, he presented me with his old instrument as a gift. I was thrilled to receive this wonderful gift, but before I even had the chance to play it, I lent it to a friend and have not seen it since. I can only hope that the chap who kept the banjo made good use of it, as it was the man's pride and joy.

Despite my date not being present, I survived, and the party was a success.

NEW YEARS EVE 1965-1966

Before I go into what happened at the end of that year, I

must mention the Lambretta Club in Salisbury. An old school friend from Ellis Robins had a Lambretta scooter, so he joined the club and persuaded me to join as well. They used to have an annual rally around the city. My friend planned to enter and persuaded me to do the same. The idea was that you invited someone to be your navigator, who would then tell you where to go.

I spent some of my free time with my cousins who lived on the other side of town in Greendale. That was where I had met the girl who failed to show for my 21st Birthday. These cousins were Neville and Wendy Woodward; their grandfather was Kenneth Carlsson, whom we had visited in Shabane some years before.

Before I entered the Lambretta Rally around Salisbury, I asked my cousin Wendy if she would ride pillion and be my navigator. Neither of us had ever done anything like this before, and as I was not familiar with the part of the city we covered, we did not do very well. However, that evening as we tried to navigate Salisbury, I saw places that I never knew existed. It was great fun, but I never did it again.

As the year drew to an end, I visited some old school friends, and we decided to get together on New Year's Eve. I invited a girl to be my date for the evening. Sadly, another guy, a good friend of mine, was put out, as he had planned to ask the same girl to be his date. Not only that, but he had no intention of asking anyone else and advised us that he would not be joining us that evening. All the same, after a lot of persuasion he agreed to attend but only on his own.

It proved to be a relatively uneventful evening. We decided that we would go to Salisbury Kopjie, overlooking the city, to see the sunrise on the New Year of 1966. Sadly, that New Year was almost a repeat of my 21st Birthday party as I left the Kopjie on my own! My friend escorted my date back to her home, and sometime later, the two of them got married.

I would ask my readers to understand that I was not in the right relationship with God at this time, and neither of these two young women was a committed Christian. Although these two events were extremely painful at the time, I know that my God was watching over me and making sure that I did not become too serious with someone who was not a believer in the Lord Jesus Christ. He made sure that I did not marry someone who may well have caused me to live a different life from the one I have subsequently lived.

MY FIRST MOTORCAR

I am not sure when it happened, but Avril came to live with us in Salisbury. She managed to get work in the city and get a lift into work with Uncle Fred. However, as already explained, he started work early, which was some time before Avril needed to be at work. Also, as Works Manager, he usually worked late, sometime after she finished work, which meant Avril was waiting around every day for a long time. So I decided to sell my much-loved motorbike and purchase a car so we could travel together to work every day.

It is quite remarkable, looking back, that I could buy the car that I ended up buying. Some years before, while living in Cape Town and riding to school on my bike, I admired the Renault Dauphine, a new model at the time. As I looked around at second-hand cars in Salisbury, I came upon a lovely red Renault Dauphine and decided to sell my bike and buy the vehicle. This car was to prove a real blessing, not only to my sister and me but also to many others who were my passengers in the days ahead.

Chapter 2

RESTORED AND PREPARED FOR THE FUTURE

It is quite clear that God had not given up on me, as the following fantastic story reveals. Despite falling away yet again, The Lord sent a man called Kenneth Mawire to remind me of His love.

KENNETH MAWIRE

I first met Kenneth when driving home along the Old Gatooma Road to 'Jabula', our home opposite the Gliding Club. When I saw him thumbing a lift, I stopped, and he had hardly sat down in my car when he began to speak to me about the Lord!

"Are you a Minister of the Gospel?" I asked

He replied, "No, I am just a member of the congregation."

"What church do you attend?" I asked

"The Assemblies of God!" was his reply.

At that point, I stopped asking questions, as I knew that I ought to be attending my own Assembly. When I discovered where he lived, some distance beyond my home, I took him all the way, as I was so convicted! However, that was not the only time that I gave him a lift. Six months to a year later, having since made right with God and back in fellowship once again, we met again.

This time, travelling down the new Bulawayo road, I saw a man hitching a lift. I stopped, and almost as soon as he got into my car, he spotted my Bible in the open glove compartment. This time he was the one asking the questions. "Are you a preacher?"

"No, I am just a member of the congregation." I replied

His next question was, "What church do you attend?"

To which I replied, "The Assemblies of God."

"I also attend the Assemblies of God," he said.

"I think that we have met before," I stated.

Once again, I took him all the way home to Gillingham Township (Dzivarasekwa) on a road that I had never travelled before. Thus, began a lifetime friendship with Kenneth, which continues to the present day. He is still preaching the Gospel even though he is over 90 years old.

THE YOUTH MEETING

As explained previously, some of us young men had drifted away from God and Christian fellowship sometime before. As a result, like most if not all 'backsliders', I tried to avoid my former Christian friends when I saw them walking down the street or anywhere else. The reason being that they usually asked difficult, often probing questions or made awkward statements like, "We have missed you. We would love to see you back at church. Why not come this weekend?"

One day, while walking down Second Street in Salisbury, I saw Alan Keeling coming towards me. He was one of the young men at the Assembly, and I hoped that he had not seen me and quickly crossed the road, planning to avoid the usual embarrassing conversation that would likely ensue. However, he had seen me and was not planning on letting me escape, so he also crossed the road. If I crossed the road again, it would be too obvious, and so I had no chance; I was trapped with no way of escape.

After exchanging greetings, Alan said, "On Friday evening, we have a special youth meeting; we plan to meet at the church. We will then be going to the home of… for a swimming evening followed by a 'braai', and it would be great if you would come. We would love to see you."

For the uninitiated, a 'braai' is the same thing as a 'barbecue'. As I had nothing planned, I agreed to attend this special youth meeting, so that Friday evening, I went to the youth meeting, and everyone present went out of their way to make me welcome. As a 'backslider', I felt like a fish out of water despite everyone enjoying themselves and despite their kind welcome. I praise God for Alan Keeling, as God was beginning His work of restoring me to fellowship with Him and with His church. So it was that at the end of the evening, I agreed to attend the Sunday evening service for the first time in many months.

AN APPOINTMENT NOT KEPT

The following day, I visited one of my 'backslidden' friends and told him what had happened and how I had agreed to attend the Sunday evening service the following day. He immediately said that he would like to come with me. He had also been considering returning to fellowship, which was a great encouragement to me and shows that many 'backslidden' believers only need a little nudge to draw them back into fellowship. Sadly, later that evening he phoned to say that he could not come as he was committed to some family gathering or something similar. I praise God that although it took years for him to get back into fellowship with God and His people, he eventually did.

Sometime later, after I was back in fellowship, I visited my friends Paul and Jonathan. When I explained to Jonathan what I had done, he said that he wished he had known, as he would have come with me. We need to remember that it is not easy for 'backsliders' to make that initial effort of getting back to church, and many of them are possibly just waiting for someone to make an effort to invite them, or take them with them, to church.

THE SUNDAY EVENING SERVICE

MCCHLERY AVENUE ASSEMBLY OF GOD.

When I returned to the Assembly, I met Charles Norton, the new Pastor, for the first time. I remember sitting in the meeting and listening to his powerful preaching. He was a very tall man. When he was preaching, he would look over his glasses at the congregation; it always looked as if he was looking straight at me!

Despite the warm welcome that I received and the Nortons' love and care, it was not as easy to get 'back to God' as it had been when I first became a Christian. Still, I was done with 'backsliding'! I was not going to turn away again; I had made up my mind that I would serve the Lord.

A LEADER IN THE YOUTH MEETINGS

When I first started going to the Assembly, there were

two different groups. The highly effective Junior Youth, led by Paul Brown, with a lot of young people attending. Then there was the Senior Youth, a smaller, less effective group, which as a young adult, I attended. However, it was a great blessing to me personally. Because there were so few of us, one night they asked me to lead the singing, most likely because I sing rather loudly. I was very self-conscious, and I just stood there, announcing the songs and not doing anything else. It is fair to say that I did not do a very good job, and they did not ask again.

Some years later, a new pastor, Bill Mundell, and his wife, Marlene, came to the Assembly, and together with the elders, he decided to merge the two youth groups. They entrusted the leadership of the new enlarged youth group to six young men in the Assembly. These young men were Paul Brown, who had led the Junior Youth, Alan Keeling, Malcolm Fraser, myself, and two others whose names escape me. I will deal with the Youth Work separately in another chapter as it plays a big part in the years of preparation for the Ministry.

We will now deal with my becoming a deacon.

THE MINISTRY OF A DEACON

It was during Bill Mundell's ministry that I was asked to be a deacon. It was a great honour, and I joined a group of faithful brothers, who included Eric Howes, Alan McGladdery, Alan Keeling, Malcolm Fraser, and there may well have been others. I want to make it very clear that it is a genuine privilege to be a deacon, and it is also a very responsible position. The Lord Jesus referred to Himself as a servant, and that is really what a deacon is;

called to serve, and I considered it a great honour.

It was at this time that my nickname stuck. There were three deacons called Alan. Someone suggested that we call Allan Keeling 'AJ', and me 'AB'. Before they could say anything more, Alan McGladdery interrupted and said that he would continue to be known as Alan! And so from that time until now, most people have known me as 'AB', and very few, until recently, have ever referred to me as Alan!

It was possibly a year or so later that Angus Anthony, who was still only a schoolboy, was also made a deacon. He lived just down the road and had already proved himself to be a very faithful young man, and despite his age, he became a deacon of the Assembly.

Brother Howes, the senior deacon, advised me of my responsibilities and gave me the key to the Deacons' Room, where we kept the rest of the church keys. There was a typed copy of the deacons' duties on the back of the door. The responsibilities included opening the church at least 30 minutes before the service, opening and closing the windows, turning the lights on and off, welcoming people at the door, giving them songbooks, showing them to a seat if necessary, and making sure that everything was in working order. Another duty was. On Saturday evenings, turning the large pews around to sit around the Lord's table for the Breaking of Bread service and replacing them after the service in preparation for the Sunday meetings.

As a deacon, I had to attend the business meeting, held at 5.30 pm on the second Monday of the month, to give the treasurer enough time to produce the monthly accounts. These were extraordinary meetings and were open to all the Assembly members if they desired to attend.

THE BUSINESS MEETING

On arrival at the business meeting, the treasurer would give us a copy of the accounts' monthly statement to examine. Someone opened the meeting in prayer at the appointed time, and the treasurer presented the monthly financial reports to those present, including the current minister, elders, deacons, and others. Some attended to advise the meeting of the needs in other Christian Ministry areas in the country.

The Assembly was well established and always received more income than it needed. After meeting the assembly's needs, there was still money left over for disposal. 'The National Development Fund' was one of the regular recipients of the Assembly's generosity. It helped to provide a living wage for the ministers of other English language Assemblies around the country. If they had a shortfall in their income, they could always make a phone call, and a cheque would be in the post. I believe that it was mainly due to this fund that we could pioneer new Assemblies throughout the country in the 1970's.

We also contributed to an equally important fund called 'The Back to God Crusade Fund', established by Nicholas Bhengu to finance the 'African' work in South Africa, Rhodesia and elsewhere. He insisted that any finance given by white churches for the work under his oversight needed to go through this fund so that his fellow black ministers did not become dependent upon handouts from the white churches. As an Assembly, we were committed to winning Rhodesia for Christ, and so every month allocated hundreds of Rhodesian Dollars to the 'The Back to God' account. Due to the fall in the Zimbabwean dollar value in recent years, it is necessary to clarify that this took place when there were two Rhodesian dollars to the British pound.

I need to mention my friend Kenneth Mawire again. After I gave him a lift on the second occasion that we met, he invited me to minister at a house meeting in his home. The first night that I attended, the room was packed to overflowing, and it was hard to see, as there was no electricity and only one gaslight. Sadly, while I was preaching, despite everyone sitting on the floor, a man in the front row was nodding off to sleep resulting in people throwing little pebbles at him to wake him up. I wonder if Billy Graham ever had people sleeping in his meetings?

I discovered that Kenneth had lost his job with Barbours, the big departmental store in Salisbury, due to sanctions, leaving him with no income. His household included his wife, children and two younger brothers, Robert and Kingston, who were still at school.

He desired to preach the Gospel, and I wanted to help him achieve his goal, so I spoke to some of my friends and asked them if they wanted to help. Then for some time after this, Alan Keeling, Malcolm Fraser, Antoinette Fourie, and possibly one or two others, including myself, chipped in R$10.00 a month to help support Kenneth fulfil his dream to preach the Gospel. We thought that we had made it very clear that what we were doing was between Kenneth, ourselves, and the Lord, and no one else. However, somehow the word got out that we were supporting him.

Some years before, the Assemblies of God in South Africa and Rhodesia had been very united. It included the American, Canadian, and British missionaries, the 'White' churches, and the 'Back to God Crusade' under Brother Bhengu. However, this had changed. As a result, the American and Canadian missionaries had gone their own way, and in time Ezekiel Gutu had established a breakaway group called the Assemblies of God Africa. AOGA was multiplying all over the country, and Kenneth was associated with them. Unwittingly we were not only supporting a black worker as an individual, but we were also helping someone who was not part of our movement!

Ezekiel Gutu saw this as a problem claiming that McChlery Avenue was now backing him by supporting one of his ministers. Our elders received a message from Brother Udd, a missionary in Malawi, who asked whether this was true? After some investigation, they discovered that we were involved, and the elders approached Alan Keeling. I escaped being spoken to, as I was not around at the time.

We needed to work closely with Brother Bhengu in Rhodesia. The elders were not all that happy, and neither was Brother Bhengu. Nevertheless, we continued to assist Kenneth but asked him not to let anyone know or else we would have to discontinue our assistance! It is interesting to note that both Kenneth's brothers, Kingston and Robert, became ministers of the Gospel and are currently in Australia or the USA. Kenneth's son, Mighty Ken Mawire, is also a preacher of the Gospel!

However, let's get back to the business meeting. Once we accounted for the church's needs and the other two funds, the chairman, usually one of the elders, would come to an item on the agenda, 'Any other business' or 'Money for disposal'. It was then that people had the opportunity to speak up, and money would be allocated to the 'Scripture Union', 'The Scripture Gift Mission', 'Youth for Christ', 'The Bible Society', 'The Leprosy Mission', and other Christian ministries.

I am so thankful that I was privileged to be part of such generosity! Sadly, many congregations are very inward-looking and spend the vast majority of their income on themselves, even if they have a large congregation. I can honestly say that this Assembly had a Kingdom Vision for the whole country.

As deacons, we had many discussions about who ought to control the Assembly's money. However, the minister and elders had made it very clear that they would continue to oversee the Assembly's finances. Despite that, most of us deacons felt that they, the minister and elders, ought to concentrate on the oversight of the spiritual needs of the Assembly and leave the deacons to oversee the practical, financial, and administrative needs of the fellowship. Despite this slight disagreement, God blessed the Assembly during those years. I look back on those years with a grateful heart and the sure knowledge that, once a deacon, always a deacon. Hallelujah!

MISSION RHODESIA

I am not sure what year this took place, but one evening I was walking down First Street in Salisbury with Geoff Kilpatrick, and we spoke about the need to evangelise all the smaller towns in the country. In many of these places, there was no Assembly and no effective Evangelical witness. As we considered the needs, we came up with a plan. The idea was to purchase a vehicle similar to a VW Camper Van and travel around the country from town to town. We would hire halls in every town we came to and conduct an evangelistic crusade. We were two earnest young men with a passion for extending the Kingdom of God. Sadly, we never took it any further, and sometime later, Geoff dropped out of fellowship, and not long afterward, we lost touch. Hopefully, Geoff found his way back to God and into Christian fellowship.

While writing this chapter, something struck me. Although I did not hold crusades in all the small towns, I was later blessed to have the opportunity to preach in many towns across Rhodesia. These towns included Wankie, Bulawayo, West Nicholson, Gwelo, Selukwe, Que Que, Redcliff, Gatooma, Salisbury, Beatrice, Fort Victoria, Sinoia, Kariba, Marandellas, Rusape, Odzi, Umtali, Juliesdale, Inyanga, Chipinga, Middle Sabi, and many others. I feel that even though we never followed up on our proclaimed plan, the Lord heard my unspoken prayer and blessed me with many opportunities. I was able to preach in most of the centres of the population right across the land, at one time or another. It may not have been as an Evangelist, but, praise God, I had the joy of leading men and women to Christ in many of those places! God is so good, hallelujah!

THE MINISTER COMES TO VISIT

Over the years, I have met many Christians who believe that their local minister has the responsibility of visiting them now and then. However, depending on the size of the congregation, this is an unrealistic expectation. During my entire Christian life, I have only had two visits from my minister, and that was when I was a member of the Assembly in Salisbury.

The first visit took place when our minister was trying to encourage house meetings to evangelise the community. Having heard what he had to say, I suggested that as my stepfather was not likely to attend the Assembly, maybe we could take the Assembly to him. As a result, Bill Mundell and a few Assembly members descended on our home at Jabula one weekday evening, which, I might add, was with my parents' full approval. Despite enjoying a good evening, my stepfather failed to change his opinion. That was the first visit!

The second visit took place when I had the flu, and I was on my own as the family was away, and I was dying. If someone has the cheek to talk about 'man flu' and that I am exaggerating, I have never been so sick in my entire life. On that occasion, I was very encouraged when John Stegman came to visit and prayed for me.

Still, before he left, he said, "Don't worry AB, my Grandmother always used to say, 'It takes an awful lot to kill weeds.'"

With those parting words ringing in my ears, he was on his way. As you have no doubt realised the 'flu' did not kill me, and I was soon back on my feet. By the way, just in case you didn't guess, John Stegman had a brilliant sense of humour, which I really appreciated, and despite his comment about what his Grandmother had to say, I respected him as a great man of God!

When I finally arrived back at the Assembly, I discovered that the flu had struck down almost the entire fellowship. I have a sneaking suspicion that I may have been the one to catch it first and could well have infected the whole fellowship. Still, that is only my theory, and it would be best that you keep it to yourself! Thanks!

THE TERRITORIAL ARMY

On returning to civilian life after completing my 4 ½ months training in The Army, my commitment to our country's defense had only just begun. Having done my initial training, I was then required to attend a regular monthly weekend parade, training exercises, and an annual camp.

I remember one weekend very well, and what happened makes very distressing reading. So if you were a captain or sergeant major in the regular army, maybe you ought to skip this section of my story. When this incident took place, I had only just been

A TRAINING EXERCISE IN RHODESIA.

promoted to Lance Corporal, a rank that proved to be the pinnacle of my military career. After being inspected and briefed, I was assigned a vehicle equipped with a radio and all the equipment necessary for a mobile communications centre. Besides me, three other signallers, one who also acted as our driver, were assigned to my unit. In my defence, I must mention that I was assigned some of the most 'interesting' characters in the company; however, that is no excuse.

We were given a map and rations and ordered to set up a signalling base at a given location. The idea was that we were to erect an aerial, as per our training, and maintain communications overnight. Sadly, when we arrived at our destination, I was persuaded by the others that it was just too difficult to erect an aerial, as per the book. So, we eventually just threw the aerial over a branch and established communications.

Finally, after having had a good look around, we decided that the only comfortable sleeping area was on a disused road, so that is where we decided to sleep. My colleagues persuaded me (you can tell that my promotion had not gone to my head) that staying up all night was just too much, and so we pretended to lose communications with our base, switched off the radio, and went to bed. How we imagined that no one would investigate what had happened, I honestly do not know.

When we were all sound asleep on the disused road around one or two in the morning, the Sergeant Major arrived, travelling down the same disused road on which we were sleeping. The Lord must have been watching over us as he could well have run over us. At the debrief the following day, there was only one unit discussed, my unit! Every point mentioned involved what we had or had not done. As you can imagine, I was not promoted to Corporal, but, surprisingly, I was not demoted on the spot!

As can be expected, we underwent an inspection every time we arrived for our weekend exercise. As the Sergeant Major went down the line, he would often draw attention to a signaller's belt or other webbing that was not looking sparkling clean by saying in a voice that only Sergeant Majors are born with, "When was that belt last cleaned? It looks terrible?"

The usual reply would be, "Yesterday, Sir!"

That may or may not have been correct; however, one day, when I was on parade, he arrived in front of me and barked out, "When last was your equipment cleaned, it looks horrible?"

My reply was, "Last month, Sir!"

That was correct, but I am pretty sure that he did not hear what I said, as he just moved on to the next man. The Lord must have been watching over me once again!

There is a saying in the army that goes like this, "Hurry Up and Wait."

It seemed that we were always having to 'hurry up,' followed by a great deal of 'waiting' before receiving our next orders, giving us plenty of time to get to know each other.

One chap in our company was always boasting about how many girlfriends he had, so one day, I foolishly suggested that he ought to introduce me to one of these many lovely girls. He took me up on that request, and one day I received a phone call from him, asking, "Hi, I have a problem and wondered if you could help me out? I have ended up with two dates tomorrow night, so I wondered if you would join us, and then the four of us could go out dining, drinking, and dancing?"

"Look, you know that I do not drink," I replied.

"No problem, you can just have a coke."

"Thanks anyway, I think it would be a bad idea as I don't dance either."

He realised that I was not the guy he was looking for, bringing our conversation to an end. I had my chance to meet one of his many girlfriends but turned him down, and he never asked me again, for which I was very grateful.

Around about the same time, my friend, Paul Black, also a signaller in the same outfit as the other chap and myself, asked me to be his best man. "Hi AB, …and I are getting married on …. We will be having a big wedding with a band and dancing, and I would like you to be my best man. Would you do that for me?"

"Hi, Paul, congratulations! I will gladly be there for you; however, I will not be drinking any alcohol, so if we can arrange for a glass of lemonade or other soft-drink to be at the head table for the toast, that will be fine." I replied.

The wedding took place as scheduled, and I arranged, with a fair bit of difficulty, for a soft drink to be at the table to participate in the toasts. Later on, after the bride and groom had appeared on the dance floor, I took the chief bridesmaid for a short dance, as was expected. I was troubled as our fellow signaller may have been at the wedding and would not have known what I was drinking when we stood up for the toasts, and there I was on the dance floor, a man that said that he did not dance!

One day I shared my concerns with Paul Brown, one of the leading young men in the Assembly. After hearing my concerns, Paul said, "AB, as Christians, we are not supposed to stand out like a sore thumb. What you did at that wedding was alright, and you should not worry about it."

That Christmas, I was on my own as my mother and stepfather were away in South Africa. One of the young women in the Assembly, Lem Scrala, kindly invited a few of us singles from the Assembly to join her and her family for Christmas lunch. While the meal was being prepared, Lem's sister's fiancé appeared with a 'yard of ale' glass filled with beer. He invited us all to have a go, and not wanting to stick out like a 'sore thumb,' I had a turn. As a 'teetotaller' when my turn came, I took the smallest sip possible and then returned the glass, and not long afterwards we were called in for lunch.

As soon as we were seated, our host proceeded to go around the table, filling everyone's wineglass. However, when he got to me, I stopped him from filling my glass and said, "No thanks, I don't drink!"

The words were no sooner out of my mouth when Lem's sister called out, "Oh yes, you do. I saw you in the garden!"

Paul Brown's advice had succeeded in getting me into a difficult situation. As a result, 'sore thumb' or not, I have avoided alcohol since that day, no matter what anyone says!

Before moving away from The Army, I have one more story to tell about an incident during the annual training camp. I had been allocated a vehicle with the standard radio equipment installed, and we had travelled initially to Inkomo Barracks, which was some distance out of Salisbury. We waited for some considerable time before moving out. While awaiting orders, I joined a small group of men who were having a conversation and heard one of them say, "You know I never swear at home. In fact, neither do I use swear words at work. It is only when I put this uniform on that I suddenly start swearing."

Several others agreed, they said the same thing, and then finally my friend Paul Black said, "It happens to all of us except him (and he pointed to me) he never swears because he is a 'holy roller'."

I was really pleased with what Paul Black had said, except for the bit about me being 'a holy roller.' I found that hard to take from one of my friends who had previously been to the Lord's house with me! However, while I was silently shining my 'halo,' we parted company to wait for orders in several tents erected nearby.

I found a place in one of the tents, but I found myself listening to a conversation coming from the next tent. The speaker said that he had no time for religion, and although he was soon to be married, he was not getting married in a church. The more I heard, the more I felt that I needed to join the conversation to set him straight, but we were awaiting orders that could come at any moment, so I procrastinated. When we finally were given the order to go to our vehicles, I realised that I had missed a fantastic opportunity. I was disappointed and asked God to give me another chance to speak to this man.

Silently shining my 'halo' again, I approached the vehicle that I had signed for, where I saw another soldier messing around with my equipment. He had a screwdriver in his hand and was unscrewing my Morse key. When I saw what was happening, I was so angry that a torrent of swear words spewed from my mouth. I was shocked at what I had just said and looked around to see if anyone was in earshot.

As mentioned earlier in my story, Paul the apostle said,

"Therefore, let him who thinks he stands take heed lest he fall." 1 Corinthians 10:12

The man in the back of my truck was a sergeant, and he needed a screw to secure his own Morse key, and he felt he could take one of mine without asking. I was shocked at what had taken place so soon after someone had drawn attention to the fact that I did not swear as a Christian.

After a successful exercise, we stopped outside a hotel in Sinoia on the way home so the signallers could get a beer. As I do not drink, I volunteered to look after the vehicles and wait for their return. As I was walking back and forth, keeping an eye on the vehicles, I noticed that I was not the only one who had stayed outside and began to talk to the other signaller. As we began to speak, I was amazed to discover that he was the man who had been talking in the tent next to mine a few days ago. God had truly been gracious; He had given me another opportunity as I requested.

This man didn't come to know the Lord at that time, but he had a change of heart, and he and his fiancée were duly married in church. Sometime later, I was amazed to discover that as an unbeliever he had volunteered and was accepted as a Sunday School teacher in the same church.

Sadly, many church leaders do not understand that specific requirements need to be met before someone is appointed to any role in the local church. For example, we need to consider how deacons were selected in the early church in Jerusalem! The apostles said,

"Therefore, brethren, seek out from among you seven men of good reputation, full of the Holy Spirit and wisdom, whom we may appoint over this business...."
Acts 6:3

I was pleased that God had used me to change his mind but sad that the church he attended had not taken him further. What a tragedy that an unbeliever was put in charge of young lives, influencing them to become unbelievers just like their teacher.

With that, we will move on to the next part of my story!

Chapter 3

THE RHODESIA RAILWAYS

My Rhodesia Railways career began straight after completing my initial Army training and ended when I entered into full-time Christian Ministry. I have included most (but possibly not all) stories relating to this period of my life.

My uncle, Cyril Stanton Robertson, was the Superintendent of the Eastern Region of the Rhodesia Railways when I began my military service. However, by the time that I completed my training in Bulawayo just 4 ½ months later, he had already retired. During his extensive career on the Railways, he had become very well-known and highly regarded by all who knew him. When I first started work, many of the men I worked with had known him, and one man said that while he was Superintendent, the Eastern Region was affectionately known as 'Robbie's Railways.'

As previously explained, I had an interview at Railway Headquarters in Bulawayo, resulting in an offer of a position as soon as I completed my military training. Thereby, my career as a railwayman began when I returned home and worked in Salisbury's Eastern Region accounts department.

On arrival at Merchant House on Forbes Avenue for my first day at work, I was taken around the office and introduced to all the staff by the chief clerk. He then instructed one of the clerks to teach me the job and keep an eye on me. All my workmates had previously been drivers, firemen, conductors, or guards. They had moved to the accounts department later in their careers, and most of them were looking forward to being pensioned off and not keen to take on extra duties.

The Railways had just introduced a massive new computer to computerise the pay-sheets. As this was all very new, we continued to do everything the old way before feeding the results into the computer.

It was an excellent office to work in, and I could not have been treated better by my workmates. The Accounts Department staff included the sub-accountant and a chief clerk. They were responsible for the department's different sections dealing with budgets, expenditure, pay-sheets, and the pay-office, which was down at the Railway Station. Besides the men, I worked with a couple of female typists and the all-important tea boy. I initially worked in pay-sheets where we calculated the entire region's staff's wages. Each clerk was responsible for calculating a specific section of the railway staff's salaries, including their basic pay, allowances, and overtime.

I enjoyed the experience of calculating the wages, but after several months I felt I needed something more challenging as I was keen to learn as much as I could. With this in mind, I approached the chief clerk to see if it was possible to move onto another section. He was amazed at my request, so amazed that he again took me around the office to advise the rest of the staff that he had never had a staff member ask for a *harder* job in all his years on the job. Despite his amazement, he granted my request, and I was moved to another section sometime later. Around that time, one of my workmates advised me that on the Railways, "The more you know, the more they ask you to do, so it is not good to know too much!"

Perhaps it was not the best advice that a young man who was just starting work needed to hear! However, it was not the only 'good advice' that I received. The next 'good advice' was given to me one day when we were doing the filing.

At the end of each month, we were required to file all the timesheets used to calculate every one's pay so that if any queries arose, we could easily find the information we needed. Most of us made sure that we produced a nice cardboard cover, cut to size, to bind everything neatly. However, one of the clerks did not bother at all. He observed quite correctly to be sure,
"No one will care how we filed these things a hundred years from now!"

Another chap assured me that he did not work for The Railways, he used to say, "I make sure that The Railways work for me."

Despite these comments, most if not all of these men did the job they were asked to do and did it well. One of the sad things about the office where I worked was that at least three men had a significant drinking problem. One of the clerks used to come to work very early in the morning (he was always at work a couple of hours before I arrived, dead on time), and then he would work flat out until lunchtime. He kept on top of his work, but sadly he was not much use after lunch as he would have been secretly consuming alcohol all morning.

Another one of the clerks with a drinking problem had a positive response when I spoke to him about the Lord Jesus. I arranged for my minister, John Stegman, to visit him at his home, where he led him to the Lord. As far as I am aware, he was set free from the curse of alcohol and from then on served the Lord with his wife in the Salvation Army, where his wife was already a member.

Another man, who was old enough to be my father, as indeed they all were, used to hide alcohol in different places at work and drink continually throughout the day. He was a bachelor, and a rather lonely man, living in the Railway single quarters. One day I persuaded him to attend the Gospel Meeting at the Assembly, and he asked the Lord Jesus into his life. Praise God! I was so concerned for his welfare that I even considered leaving home to live in single quarters to keep an eye on him.

My home Assembly was a very good fellowship, and I cannot speak more highly of this congregation which made an incredible impression on my early Christian life. However, one of the things that worried me at the time was that none of the older folk in the Assembly befriended my workmate. Sadly, this may well have contributed to the fact that he gradually drifted away. I never did move to single quarters, and not long afterwards he went back to his drinking ways. I continued to try and help him, and on several occasions at work, I even poured his bottle of Brandy or Vodka down the sink in my efforts to keep him off the bottle, but it did not do much good.

Sadly, not long afterwards he stopped coming to the Assembly and then stopped coming to work and finally must have lost his job. He moved out of single quarters, and I lost touch with him. After making a lot of effort to locate him, I think he phoned me at work and gave me his address. As soon as I could, I visited him but found him totally 'wasted.' As I looked at him, my heart went out to him, but I could not help him. As I looked around the room, I spotted a half-empty bottle of Brandy under the bed and reached down and picked it up and said, "Ron, I want to help you, but I cannot do so unless you are willing to help yourself. Today I am offering you a choice. You can have this half-empty bottle of Brandy or have my friendship and help. What will it be?"

Sadly, his reply was, "Pass me the bottle."

I left, and sometime later, I heard that he had been deported from Rhodesia as an habitual drunkard and sent back to the UK. As I look back upon this incident, I am aware that I possibly could have done more to assist my friend; however, at the time, I felt that there was no more that I could do.

Not all my workmates had problems with alcohol. Another one of those who was a heavy drinker, not an alcoholic as far as I was aware, was a man who had been a mercenary in the Congo in the days shortly after Belgium had handed over control of what had been The Belgium Congo to the locals.

The Belgium Congo became independent as the Republic of the Congo on the 30th June 1960. On that day, Belgium handed over the country's control to the locals, and Patrice Lumumba became its first prime minister. The country was far from ready to take back control of state affairs. During the chaos that followed, another man, Moise Tshombe, seized control of the copper-rich Katanga province and proclaimed its independence from the rest of the country.

In his endeavours he recruited a small army of white mercenaries composed of British, Rhodesian, French and South Africans to bolster his armed forces.

My workmate signed up and served under Major Hoare, an ex-British Army man better known as 'Mad Mike' Hoare. These mercenaries assisted Katanga in its 'rebellion,' until, largely due to international pressure, it was finally defeated and reabsorbed into the Republic of the Congo.

In 1964, The Congolese Prime Minister asked Major Hoare to form and lead a military unit called the 5th Commando, which helped save 1,600 civilians (mostly European missionaries) from Stanleyville during the Simba rebellion. This incredibly violent group of rebels were responsible for much bloodshed in those turbulent years. Sadly, in putting down the revolution, the Congolese armed forces were, possibly, as evil or almost as evil as the rebels in their indiscriminate slaughter of civilians.

The Congo Evangelistic Mission was a large Mission supported by the Elim Pentecostal Church and the British Assemblies of God who ministered in the congo.

A few years before I became a member of the Assembly in Salisbury, they provided food, clothing, and accommodation for many CEM missionaries as they prayed about their future because many had to leave the Congo during those turbulent years with little more than the clothes on their backs.

The sad story of the Congo's chaos was one of the main reasons why the vast majority of white Rhodesians were unwilling to accept 'majority rule' in the 1960s. They were also concerned that the Soviet Union and the Chinese Communists, who supported every Black Nationalist Movement that existed, were contributing to the rapid spread of Communism sweeping down Africa at the time.

One day, back in the office, my ex-mercenary workmate and I had a conversation during which he said, "You don't smoke, drink, and don't womanise; what do you get out of life?"

I do not remember how I responded to what he said. He was not a happy man despite all his bravado.

He ought to have read what Solomon said many years ago, "Let us hear the conclusion of the whole matter: Fear God and keep His commandments, for this is man's all. For God will bring every work into judgment, including every secret thing, whether good or evil." Ecclesiastes 12: 13-14

I am sure that he had witnessed many terrible things in the Congo during that turbulent time, which would naturally have had a significant influence on his life. Because he did not know Jesus Christ as his Lord and Saviour, and therefore had no hope of eternal life, one could understand his philosophy of, "Let us eat and drink, for tomorrow we die." 1 Corinthians 15.32 b

Despite understanding to some degree where this man was coming from, he and others like him have no excuse. The Bible, that amazing book, was freely available. Many good Churches existed all over the City, proclaiming The Gospel in so many different ways. It was true then, and it is still true today.

The answer was, and still remains, that men and women need to turn to God, just like Solomon said!

The Lord has promised in His Word, the Bible, that if we seek Him, we will find Him. There is no other way to be ready for eternity other than accepting the way of Salvation that God has provided. The Lord Jesus is the only hope for man, and we all need to receive Him as our Lord and Saviour.

One morning when I arrived at work, I discovered that someone, most likely the man we have been discussing, had put a large picture of a naked woman on his office wall. I was not impressed, and although he had not put it on my office wall, his office was one of several rooms with three desks. I promptly took it down, much to everyone's surprise. When I look back on this incident, I am amazed at the boldness the Lord gave me, and amazingly the picture remained down!

Another character that I worked with was a man who was unashamedly homosexual. He was a very nice person in many ways, and we often discussed the Bible, but he never showed any desire to change his life and receive the Lord as his Saviour. He told me that his parents were not married but had produced a large family and never saw any reason to get married. One day he appeared in the office looking much the worse for wear, having been beaten up by his partner. He also informed me that Cecil John Rhodes had permitted a club to operate in Salisbury for those who were homosexual even in the early days.There is a lot that I could say about his parents' decision not to get married, and also about his lifestyle.

I will turn to the Bible and let Paul the apostle take the floor, "For this reason God gave them up to vile passions. For even their woman exchanged the natural use for what is against nature. Likewise, the men, leaving the natural use of the woman, burned in their lust for one another, men with men committing what is shameful and receiving in themselves the penalty of their error which was due. And even as they did not like to retain God in their knowledge, God gave them over to a debased mind, to do those things which are not fitting;...." Romans 1:26-28

Returning to the men I worked with, I shared an office with a Portuguese man who had an interesting habit that I observed every day. It began with a trip to the toilet, where he would wash his hands thoroughly just before we had a tea break. On his return to the office, he would bring out a tin where he kept a chocolate bar. After taking the chocolate bar out, he would carefully break off one piece and put the bar back in the tin, and return it to its place in the top drawer of his desk. Now and then, he would be overcome with generosity and pass a single piece of chocolate to me, which I, of course, would not refuse. I found it particularly strange to witness this daily ritual because I would eat a whole bar of chocolate, not just a single piece. He must have been a man with tremendous control over his desires!!

Another chap, in fact, the man who had first instructed me on the job, had also developed his particular little ritual. Sometime during most days, he would take a lovely green cucumber out of his drawer and eat it with a little salt. On occasions, he shared the cucumber with me. I must say that it was lovely on a hot day to partake of some nice 'cool' cucumber. Sadly, I am scratching my head to remember when I shared anything with my workmates. Maybe I was less generous than the rest of them!

At the end of each month, it was naturally important that the 'books' balanced and on occasion, we would have a problem. Something would be wrong, and we usually found the problem in a certain man's section. He was a lecturer at the Salisbury Polytechnic College, and he once told me that his life began at 4:30 pm when he left our office. He was well qualified, and the rumour was that he was killing himself by degrees! Nevertheless, well-educated or not, whenever we could not balance the books, the problem was usually to be found in his section.

We all got on surprisingly well, for which I praise God. As you may well have picked up while reading my story, I have always enjoyed a good joke, and there were usually a good number of jokes told in our office. However, I do object to dirty jokes, jokes below the belt, and all of the men in the department were well aware of my feelings, but they were also fond of pulling my leg, and I would often be confronted by someone calling me over and saying, "Hi Robbie, do you want to hear a good joke?"

To which I would usually reply, "Only if it is a clean joke!"

One day we got a new member of staff, an attractive young woman, employed as a typist, and although she did not work for our section, the men encouraged her to visit now and then. They quickly discovered that, like our Polytechnic Lecturer, she also had another job. She worked as a dancer at a local nightclub, so they persuaded her to bring in her dress for them to see. They made a point of making sure that I saw it too. It left nothing to the imagination!

There was a large walk-in safe and filing cabinet in the passage between the offices where the more important documents were stored. One day some of my workmates contrived to get this young woman and myself into the safe at the same time, at which point they shut the door and turned off the lights. Neither of us was amused to be locked up together in the safe. Praise God! They released us quickly. In a strange way, it did reveal that they respected the things I stood for.

Although we had very little to do with them in our office routine, there were two other women that I want to mention who worked in our offices. The one was an older lady whom I discovered had been a member of my local Assembly. Sadly, she had been hurt by something years before and had not got over the upset. I encouraged her to forgive and get back into fellowship, but she refused to do so.

How sad it is that many men and women find it very difficult to forgive. When we consider what Jesus endured on the Cross of Calvary to save our souls, why is it that so many fail to heed His Word? Did He not say the following words in the verses that follow in what is usually referred to as the Lord's Prayer?

"For if you forgive men their trespasses, your heavenly Father will also forgive you. But if you do not forgive men their trespasses, neither will your Father forgive your trespasses." Matthew 6:14-15

This truth is so powerful, so if today you are struggling to forgive, ask God for help. It is extremely important; do not rest until you have made a point, with God's help, to forgive all who have wronged you!

The other woman was a lot younger, more my age. She was a lovely girl, and when I was 'backslidden', we went on a date one evening to the Drive-in Cinema. I was amazed some years later to discover, when I was the minister at McChlery Avenue Assembly, that she and her husband and family were part of my congregation.

Yet another staff member was a practising Roman

Catholic, and during the years that we worked together, we had many discussions. One day I was quite excited when he told me that he had made a plan of preparing for eternity. He estimated he would most likely live for another 20 years or so, and so as of that day, he was going to prepare himself for heaven. Having heard what he had to say, I then said, "That's great; however, have you not forgotten something? You could die tomorrow, and you would not be ready for another twenty years, according to you. The Bible tells us that we can be ready today if we are willing to accept the Lord Jesus as our Saviour."

Sadly, he just could not understand that Salvation is a gift from God, not something we have to earn! The Scriptures reveal that we can know that we have eternal life right now, not because of what we have done but because of what the Lord Jesus did at Calvary.

"And this is the testimony; that God has given us eternal life, and this life is in His Son. He who has the Son has life; he who does not have the Son of God does not have life. These things I have written to you who believe in the name of the Son of God, that you may know that you have eternal life, and that you may continue to believe in the name of the Son of God."
1 John 5:11-13

One last story involves a particularly grumpy member of staff. He never said "good morning" to anyone when he arrived for work, and he always seemed to be angry.

He worked in expenditures, and one day he just came in and helped himself to my files. When I discovered what he had done, I expressed my anger to the two staff members in my office. I mentioned how miserable he was and commented that he never even said "good morning" when he arrived at work. All the time I complained, one of my fellow workers was trying to make me stop by pointing to the open door which led into the culprit's room. When I finally realised what he was trying to tell me, I finished off by saying, "Too bad, it's time he heard the truth, and he ought not to take my files without asking."

Having let off a bit of steam, I then shut the door and got down to work. The amazing thing was that the following morning when he came into work, he leaned into the office and cheerfully said, "Good morning, gentlemen!"

Even more amazing was that years later, I met him at Resthaven, a Christian retreat centre outside Salisbury, where he informed me that he was now a 'born-again believer'. He had never shown any interest in the things of God, I certainly cannot claim any credit for his change of heart, but I praise God that we will be spending eternity together in the presence of God.

Although I never planned to become a 'railway man,' my Railway years were, all in all, very satisfying. One of the most enjoyable and exciting parts of our job was to do the pay run every month. Depending upon which pay run you did would naturally depend upon who you needed to pay. It would sometimes mean travelling down the railway line on one of those little motorised cars to pay gangs of men working up and down the line or by car to some isolated stations in the Railways' Eastern Region. On yet other occasions, one could be sent to the workshops or asked to assist at the pay office not far from where our offices were situated. No matter what pay run you were required to do, it meant paying out many thousands of Rhodesian Dollars in cash.

First thing on Pay Day, we collected the money for whatever pay run we needed to do. The cash would need to be signed for and then placed in a metal strongbox which was then securely locked. The man in charge (which was never me as I was a junior clerk) carried a revolver so that he could protect the cash in the event of a hold-up. However, each of the men in charge, whom I travelled with, felt safer to leave the weapon locked up with the cash. They were not keen to risk their lives defending the Rhodesia Railways property, particularly when most of them were not far off going on pension. Praise God, we never had a 'hold up,' and so always concluded our pay run satisfactorily.

I have always loved reading and would often take a book with me to work. I planned to spend time reading my book during the lunch hour. However, on this particular day, I realised that I was on top of my work during the morning and decided not to waste my day but instead spend it reading a few chapters of the book that I had brought with me. Unfortunately, before I had read more than a couple of pages, the chief clerk walked in and discovered me unashamedly immersed in a novel during office hours. As expected, he was not impressed and sent me down to the pay office to assist the paymaster. I learned that day that it was acceptable to 'pretend to be busy' when you were on top of your work, but it was not permitted to read a good book. I realised that I was wrong and learnt a good lesson that day.

There was always something of interest happening in our office, yet the following incident is such an unlikely story. I assure you that it took place. It involved a new staff member, a young man sent to me to learn the ropes.

When the chief clerk brought him through to my office, he introduced me as Mr. Robertson and him as Mr. Visser. The Chief clerk instructed me to show Mr. Visser the ropes and left me to get on with it. The staff member who warned me that "the more you know, the more they want you to do" was proved right. I had been the youngest member of staff until then, but I had asked for new challenges, which resulted in me showing this new man how to do the job!

After my boss left the room, I told the new man that the rest of the staff generally referred to me as Robbie, and I would be happy if he did the same. I then asked him what his first name was. I have no idea why he decided to pull my leg, having only just met me; however, he told me that his first name was Willoughby. I was so taken aback when he told me his name that I could not help myself and roared with laughter, to which he responded in a very hurt tone of voice by saying, "I didn't laugh when you told me your name."

I apologised and then said that his surname indicated he was Afrikaans, and Willoughby was a very aristocratic English name. Willoughby Visser just did not sound right. I then asked him how in the world he came to be called Willoughby?

He replied , "When I was born, my father worked for Volkswagen and wanted his son to have the initials VW because he was so impressed with the VWs and loved working for the company. However, this was not possible as our surname was Visser, so he chose the next best thing and called me Willoughby Visser or WV."

He had such a straight face and spoke so

convincingly that I was utterly taken in. After hearing his story, I apologised yet again and set about teaching him the job. Some weeks later, I discovered his real name and how I had been taken in by our new staff member.

My trainee was out of the office when I discovered that I needed him for something or other, so I went into the other offices looking for him. When I asked the other staff members whether they had seen Willoughby, they all replied in surprised tones, "Who is Willoughby?"

It was my turn to be surprised, and I thought they were joking with me, which was not entirely unexpected as they did it regularly. I replied that they knew perfectly well who he was, as Willoughby was the chap who was working with me. At that, they were even more puzzled and said, "His name is not "Willoughby. It's Steve!"

Because I had been so thoroughly taken in, I did not believe that his name was Steve until we had a look at his payslip, which was easy to do as if you remember, we were in the section dealing with pay sheets. It was only then that I discovered that his name was Stefanis Hermanos Jacobus Visser. As I do not have his payslip in front of me now, I am not sure that I have remembered all his names correctly or the correct spelling; however, his name was an Afrikaans name through and through. Despite his Dad supposedly having worked for VW and wanting to name him Willoughby!

I discovered that my new workmate Steve was a bit of a joker, and after that, we often shared a joke or two. However, one day he decided to tell several anti-Semitic jokes to myself and another staff member one after another. After he had shared something like the third or fourth such joke, in quick succession, the other member of staff in our office (an older man) engaged him in conversation, "Steve, do you know what the three smallest books in the world are?"

Steve was not able to answer, so my workmate said, "The first one is the Egyptian Book of War Heroes."

This was well appreciated as you have to understand that the incident that I am relating took place shortly after the six-day war in June 1967. Most white Rhodesians and many black people were fully supportive of Israel. Our news broadcasts had been full of pictures of the victorious Israeli Defence Forces and the fleeing Egyptian Army.

He then went on to say, "The second one is The Sahara Book of Waterfalls." (not the real name, but I felt that I could not include it in my book as it was not funny but very, very sad, so I came up with another title for this book.)

He concluded by saying, "The third-smallest book in the world is The Afrikaans Book Of Knowledge."

When he said that, I nearly doubled up with laughter, and to his credit, Steve did manage to crack a smile. A short while before, Steve had been enjoying himself telling inappropriate jokes at the expense of the Jewish people. Now the tables were turned, with fun being made of his people, the Afrikaners. I do not think Steve ever picked on the Jews again in our office, and of course, we did not pick on the Afrikaners. Many of my very dear friends were and indeed are Afrikaners. I will not say that we never told jokes about a certain 'Van der Merwe', as that would have been a little too much to ask. I have to conclude that you are missing some good stories for those who have never heard a 'Van der

Merwe' joke.

Before leaving my good friend Steve, I would like to share two more stories that involve him. For a short time, as already mentioned in my tale, I belonged to the Lambretta Club, although I possessed a Honda 150 Motorbike. An old school friend of mine had persuaded me to join, and because I had such a small bike, they accepted me into membership. They had a small clubhouse on the sixth floor of an office block.

One lunch hour Steve and I went to the club to play table tennis as they had a large table tennis table in one of the rooms. Some staff members saw us leaving on my motorcycle as we left to go to the club. I did not have a key, but we were given access by some other members who were present when we arrived. We had a great game, but when it was time to go back to work, we discovered that we were on our own and locked inside the building. The other members had left, locked up, and gone, having forgotten about us, or perhaps they thought that we had a key. We tried everything to get out and even considered trying to climb out of the window even though the club was on the sixth floor. It was around 5:00 pm when thankfully, we eventually got out when some other members arrived.

As you can imagine, we were missed when we failed to appear back at the office after lunch. Concerned, the chief clerk phoned the police and the hospital, thinking we may have had an accident. By the time we left the clubhouse, our whole department had already packed up and gone home. They were all relieved when we both arrived in the morning, and after being reprimanded, we got back to work.

One Sunday evening, I persuaded Steve to attend

the Gospel Meeting at the Assembly. After the meeting, we had a long chat sitting in my car outside his abode. He was on the brink of giving his life to Jesus and indeed said that he would do so before going to sleep that night. However, when I saw him in the morning, he avoided meeting up with me, and I knew that he had failed to do what he had said he would. I do trust that he did so later in his life.

During my Railway career, I was privileged to spend time working in the pay-sheets, expenditure and budget departments. One day we were asked to advise the whole region on filling in various documents to line up with the new Railway Computer. As part of the job, I was sent out with two others to visit the multiple stations on a specific section of the line. Other members of staff were despatched along different sections of track so that we covered the entire region. It was a great day out, and after we had instructed each station master how to 'feed' the computer, my workmates headed for the closest watering hole; however, it was not water that they enjoyed. After one visit and drinking coke or something similar, I just waited in the car for them to return. Strangely enough, I was once again the passenger of a driver who had been consuming more and more alcohol.

It was a real privilege to work in the budget section as I learned a lot about the need for advanced planning in an organisation like the Railways. I also had the opportunity to sit in on some of the meetings with senior staff members, where I heard them making major plans and discussing the cost of these projects.

Because Rhodesia Railways was such a significant employer and handled such large amounts of money, the Eastern Region operated two accounts at the Reserve Bank of Rhodesia. When payday was approaching, a large sum of money was sent from Head Office in Bulawayo to pay all the staff in our region, which was drawn out of the bank by the Pay Master, who then paid out this large amount of cash on payday, as I have described earlier. It was, of course, vital to pay the cheque into the correct account, or else the one account would be terribly overdrawn and potentially involve a significant overdraft fee.

One day, while working in a particular part of our department while another staff member was on leave, I was required to do this transaction. I regrettably put the cheque worth hundreds of thousands of Rhodesian Dollars into the wrong account by mistake. A few days later, the sub-accountant called me in and revealed my error. While I waited in a fair amount of trepidation, he called the Reserve Bank, who assured him that all was well as they had spotted and corrected my error. Once again, my God had sent His angels to watch over me!

While working in this particular office, I came in the door one day when two of my workmates were conversing. As I opened the door, I heard them say, "There is no such thing as a true Christian!"

What a thing to hear when you have lived and worked among all of them for so long; it was rather distressing. These colleagues felt that way because of a Christian who had previously worked in that office. They told me that he was always preaching to his fellow workmates but sadly failed to do his job correctly. Nevertheless, to hear such a statement was a real challenge to me!

During the years that I worked in that

department, I made myself available to house-sit, on many occasions, for different people when they went on holiday, including the home of the man to whom I have just referred. He and his wife had a lovely house in a good part of the town, and they asked me to look after their home for two or three weeks while they were away. I never charged anything, but if I remember correctly, they returned with some presents for me in appreciation for what I had done.

My boss, Mr. Pengelly, also asked me to look after his house while he and his wife went away. I cannot remember his home, but I remember that he had a lovely car. It was when I was having major car problems. He gave me the use of his car, and when I said that I would only use it around town and not use it over the Rhodes and Founders weekend, he was insistent that I used his car. What a privilege! I used it to go to a youth camp in Odzi, which was about a hundred miles out of Salisbury.

One day, while driving his car, I approached the busy intersection of Jameson Avenue and Enterprise Road when the robots turned red. I put my foot on the brakes, and absolutely nothing happened; I just carried on going. Praise God! The Lord was watching over me as nothing was coming the other way, which was something of a miracle. I made my way very slowly to a friend's house who lived nearby, and we discovered that the brake fluid had drained entirely away as the brake cable had broken. Praise God, the car was soon repaired and was a great blessing over the Rhodes and Founders weekend. The Pengellys were just as appreciative as my other workmate and his wife had been.

Because of the contrast of how unbelievers treated me when I was house-sitting, I have included the following story of how a believer treated me to encourage Christians to be generous as, sadly, I have met too many tight Christians during my life. On this occasion, A Christian and senior leader in the Assembly asked me to house-sit for him. This man almost charged me rent for looking after his house, although I had given up having tea in bed brought to me every morning by my mother and having my meals cooked for me every day! The contrast between my unsaved workmates' appreciation and generosity and my brother in Christ was remarkable. I believe that we should all be much more generous in particular to one another.

Did not our Lord say, "Give, and it will be given to you; good measure, pressed down, shaken together, and running over will be put into your bosom. For with the measure that you use, it will be measured back to you." Luke 6.38

I must share a story to do with my pay-packet when I first began work on the Railways. If you remember, I had a very good friend, Helge Schneemann, who started work sometime before me and was working in the retail trade for a hard-headed businessman and earning very little money. Well, Helge was not all that happy when he discovered that I was making more money than him from the day that I started work, even though he had been working for at least two years. As a result, he decided that it was time to look for another job, and not long afterwards he left for South Africa.

The last I heard of him was very encouraging, as he had been promoted to a senior position very soon after he moved to South Africa. Despite his low pay in Salisbury, he was well-trained, which resulted in his rapid promotion. He also came to know the Lord as his

Saviour and became an active member of a Baptist Church for which I praise God.

Although I earned more than my friend Helge, I made much less than my workmates, despite us doing the same job. Amazingly, these men encouraged me to put in for a 'special' increase not long after I started work. Over the next few years, I received the annual increases and two or possibly three 'special' increases, which thinking back, was quite extraordinary and showed my workmates concern for me and even more God's blessing upon my life. I never told Helge of my 'special' increases as he had by that time already left town.

As time went on, I became increasingly aware that I did not know enough of the Bible to enter the ministry. Having a busy life with a full-time job and all that I was involved in at the Assembly, I had precious little time to study, so I considered ways I could find time to read and learn.

After making enquiries, I concluded that if I acquired a job at the Telephone Exchange where I would be required to work shifts, I might find time outside working hours to study. With this in mind, I planned to hand in my notice and possibly actually did so.

To my horror, when my mother discovered what I was doing, she phoned my boss at work to ask him to intervene and stop me from leaving the Railways. I was upset when my boss, Mr. Pengelly, called me in for a conversation and told me, "Your Mother phoned me...."

I was around 26 years of age and was highly embarrassed that my mother had phoned my boss. In hindsight, her intervention saved me from making a huge mistake. My boss suggested that if I wanted to do shift work, I would be better off remaining on the Railways and changing my job as I would continue to earn the same salary. Following a conversation with him, I stayed on the Railways, and I think it was at that stage that I ended up in the Budgets Department.

Despite my never wanting to be a Railway man and despite my efforts to leave on several occasions, I remained on the Railways until a couple of months before the Lord opened the door for me to enter full-time Christian Ministry on Easter Sunday 1972.

Chapter 4

YOUTH WORK

THE YOUTH MEETING

It was early in 1966 when I became involved in the Youth Work at my local Assembly of God Church in Eastlea in Salisbury. I had just turned twenty-one, and I continued to be involved in the Youth Work until I entered the ministry on Easter Sunday in 1972. By this time, I was quite a lot older than most of our young people. One of the young people, possibly Chris Willis, suggested that I was getting a little too old for the youth meeting, which was confirmed when I gave a lift to two teenage girls, and while talking about a young man, I heard one of them say, "He's far too old; he's twenty-six!"

Having heard that comment, I responded by saying, "Too old? How old do you think I am?"

I think that they were a little embarrassed, and they failed to reply, and so I said, "I am already 27!"

Sad to say, they were possibly correct; I was getting a little too old for the youth meeting! However, most of the time I was involved with our youth group, I was either one of the six leaders of the youth work or the youth leader. My main reason for attending was to help lead the Youth meetings and care for the Assembly's youth.

I believe that it is true to say that God was gracious during most of that time and was pleased to bless our youth meetings, and I am sure that they made a great impression upon the young people who attended. Our meetings were not all fun and games, as is sadly the case with many church youth groups. We did have Bible quizzes, testimony times, travelling suppers, and 'braai' evenings which were all well attended and enjoyed by all. However, most of the time, we concentrated on times of praise and worship, opportunities for preaching, and beautiful times of fellowship. The meetings were designed to reach young people for Jesus Christ and encourage them to continue serving him for the rest of their lives.

I believe that our meetings became known as such. One of the reasons that young people came to the meetings was to get closer to the Lord, which was confirmed one evening when I went to pick up two young guys for the meeting. When I arrived, one of the chap's sisters asked if she could come along as well. As there was room in my car, I encouraged her to come. On our way to the meeting, I asked her why she wanted to come, and she replied without hesitation,

"I want to get to know the Lord," she said.

You can imagine how encouraging it was for me to hear her say that, and praise God, that very night she came to know the Lord as her Saviour. When I was the minister at the Hatfield Assembly some years later, she was one of our most faithful members. The last I heard, she was still faithfully serving the Lord.

If the young people did not get saved at the youth meeting, many got saved at the Sunday evening Gospel Meeting. These meetings were anointed Evangelistic Services, in particular during the ministry of Bill Mundell and John Stegman. Almost every week, we saw people respond to the Gospel message and come to know the Lord Jesus as their Saviour.

After the meetings, we often ended up at the Gremlin, a drive-in restaurant not far from the church, and pack out a little room that they had there, for an hour or so, before heading home. Les and Avril Helen ran the Gremlin for some years, and we were regular customers. When he operated the Gremlin, Les allowed an advertising company to place a sizeable illuminated advertising board above his premises. When it was operating, various adverts would appear one by one. Part of the deal allowed him to advertise his restaurant, but he also included one for the Assembly.

One Monday morning I discovered that the advert worked, as one of my workmates called out to me as I arrived at work, "Robbie, I just can't escape from you inviting me to your Church. You even followed me to the Gremlin last night!"

I believe that we all enjoyed our times at the Gremlin; however, strangely enough, when we came to pay for our coffees or cold drinks, there always seemed to be a shortfall after everyone had put in their contributions. As a result, my coffee always cost me more than the menu price, as I regularly ended up contributing to the shortfall. After some weeks of this, I decided that I had had enough, so when I left home for the meeting, I purposely left my wallet behind and only took enough money with me to pay for my drink.

Due to car problems, I ended up borrowing an old Fiat 600 from my stepfather. After a while, as I was using it all the time, I suggested that instead of borrowing the car, it would be better if I bought it from him, and a few days before this incident, we concluded the deal. I went out of my way to give lifts to those who wanted to attend the meetings. That evening I had given a ride to Cheryl

Cormack, who stayed with her sister, Maureen, in Mabelreign, not too far from where we lived.

On our way home, near a garage in Belvedere, the car stopped and would not start again. It was serious, as I was later to discover, and would need a complete engine overhaul. Had I been on my own, I would have just parked the car, abandoned it and walked the five or so miles home. However, I still needed to get Cheryl home but had no money on me as I had left my wallet at home on purpose. As I was in a bit of a predicament, I turned to Cheryl and said, "Cheryl, we will need to get a taxi to get you home, but I have left my wallet at home. Do you have any money I could borrow until I can pay you back?"

Her reply was not encouraging, so I hired a taxi to take us home. Instead of paying a little extra for someone's coffee that evening, I ended up paying a lot more for a taxi to take me home. Perhaps there is a lesson to be learned here?

Returning to the youth, besides the Gremlin, another favourite was the 'Coffee Squashes' we enjoyed at different people's homes. They were great times when we enjoyed each other's company and great singsongs. There was usually someone available to play the guitar, and we loved to sing all the wonderful songs that we were singing at the Assembly. The amount of available food depended on the home we invaded. At one of these 'Coffee Squashes,' I was offered a second coffee, and as I had enjoyed the first, I accepted a second, and that night I just could not sleep, so ever since I have been careful about how much coffee I consume before going to bed. They were great times of close fellowship and are still remembered by many even though they took place so many years ago.

As a group, we also enjoyed outings to various places around Salisbury, including the fantastic granite rock formations at Domboshawa and the Balancing Rocks at Epworth. Then there was Mermaids Pool, Lake McIlwaine, and Ewanrigg Botanical Gardens. On occasions, we arranged a game of football or rounders, which we all enjoyed. During these games, I discovered some of my friends' competitive nature, particularly Alan Keeling and Malcolm Fraser. There could be no doubt that whatever we played, they were out to WIN! It seemed that for Alan and Malcolm, the game was always very serious!

Some years later, I started playing squash with a Canadian missionary with whom I became friends. When I mentioned it to Malcolm Fraser, a keen tennis player, he was eager to have a go, so I arranged a time when we could play. However, before we played, Malcolm told me that he had either never played squash or that it was such a long time since he had played that he had forgotten the rules, so I would have to teach him the game. Well, after we played a few games together, he beat me so badly that I never suggested we play again. Sad to say, my missionary friend also stopped playing with me, as I fear I was just not up to his standard. Well, you can't win them all, can you?

There was one occasion that was quite significant for our youth group. We had gone to a nearby park to play rounders when a couple of local boys arrived on the scene and stood around watching. We encouraged them to join in, and later they attended the youth meetings. They also attended the youth camp soon after, where they committed their lives to the Lord. Praise God that whatever we do can be used to evangelise the lost.

As can be expected, we did have several budding romances among the youth, but it often led to difficulties when they broke up. It must have been shortly after one of these 'break-ups' that we attended a meeting at another church, and on our way home, we went to another drive-in restaurant before returning to the Assembly. I had a carload as usual, and on our return, one of the girls remained seated for some time and did not seem to want to leave. She kept looking at another car across the car park where her former boyfriend and his latest were still talking.

However, I was shocked when this lovely Christian young woman said with real conviction, "I hate her!"

When I heard the words, which came out of her mouth, I said with equal conviction, "You cannot hate her. You are a Christian!"

She repeated what she had said with added emphasis, "I truly hate her!"

Having heard what she said, we spent a long time talking together, until long after her ex-boyfriend had departed. A few days later, I was concerned and arranged for both girls to meet with me at the Assembly. Our minister, John Stegman, was happy to let me get on with it but gave me all the support that I needed.

I spent some time talking to both of them, emphasizing the importance of not allowing bitterness and hatred to enter their lives. I encouraged them to forgive each other, saying how we could not expect God's forgiveness if we are unwilling to forgive each other? I then suggested that it was time to pray and ask God's forgiveness and help. I made it clear that I expected to hear them both pray aloud, after which I would pray for them both.

It was not long before the first girl prayed, but it was a long time before the other girl was able to open her mouth and pray. I only prayed after I had heard both of them pray. As far as I am aware, they never became the best of friends, but I firmly believed it was vital for both of them and all our youth that they forgive one another no matter what had taken place.

The Lord Jesus clearly taught that, "By this all will know that you are My disciples, if you have love for one another." John 13:35

On a lighter note, one day, I needed to phone Ricky De Lacy, one of our young people, who lived with his parents on the opposite side of town from where I was living. His mother answered the phone, and while she went to call her son, I was amazed to find myself listening to a conversation between two young women. Somehow, we had a crossed line, and I was able to listen to their conversation quite clearly. Not only did I recognise who they were, but believe it or not, my name came up in their conversation. By the time Ricky answered the phone, they had hung up.

That Friday night at the Youth meeting, I told the story to all the young people. You can imagine how shocked they were to discover that I had listened to their conversation on the telephone without them knowing. However, I assured them that what I had heard, including their mention of myself, was not a problem. Hopefully, it was a warning to us that we need to be careful about what we discuss on the telephone as we never know who could be listening. If that was true all those years ago, how much more so in 2020?

It was relatively easy having a meeting at the Assembly but having a 'braai' or a swimming evening at someone's home created challenges. One was making sure that everyone got home at an acceptable hour. For the older youth, that was not a problem as many of them worked and some had their own transport. The problem was usually with those who were still at school and needed a lift home. The City of Salisbury was vast, and those available to provide lifts were few, often creating a problem getting everyone home. There was petrol rationing at this time as well.

One Friday evening, I realised that to get all those home who needed a lift, I would need to make two trips. My first trip would involve giving a ride to anyone who lived furthest from where I lived, and my second trip would include providing a lift to those who lived on my side of the City. However, by the time I dropped off the last of my passengers, a lovely 14-year-old girl, it was after 10:00 pm, and her father had been very concerned, as he expected her home a lot sooner than that.

You need to understand that there were no mobile phones in those days and so when I arrived home close to 11:00 pm my Mother told me that John Stegman, my minister, had phoned sometime before. When he discovered that I was still not home, he asked that I call him as soon as I returned. I did so but was rather annoyed to discover that the father of the girl I had just dropped off at home had telephoned him sometime before. He was concerned about his daughter, who was still not home, and it was then after 10:00 pm. I explained the challenge with lifts and that I had travelled many miles that evening dropping off people, and that I got her home just as soon as I could.

However, the thing that really annoyed me was that this man's daughter was with me, AB Robertson, and so what was he worried about!!

As I look back on this event, I praise God for fathers concerned for their daughters, fathers who watch over their daughters to protect them in this evil world. There are too few parents who are involved in their children's lives! Too few parents love their sons and daughters enough to set down rules that they expect their children to obey. Although I was annoyed that evening, as I felt they were questioning my reputation, I praise God for a father who cared!

My next story will sound like a detective story and reveals something of the demanding nature of youth work! The doors of Christian meetings are always open, inviting whosoever, and we should not be surprised if some interesting characters come through the doors.

Before I left home, I had a phone call from a young woman I had arranged to pick up for the Friday youth meeting. She told me that a young woman, we both knew, had asked if she and her newly married husband could stay the weekend with her in her one bedroomed flat. She had agreed, on the understanding that it was only for two nights, as she wasn't supposed to have guests. She had invited them to the meeting that night and asked if I would give all three of them a lift.

I duly arrived to pick them up, and we set out for the meeting. We came across a couple of ladies standing next to an old Morris Minor, which had broken down. Having ascertained that my passenger, the young man who I had only just met, was a bit of a mechanic, we pulled over and offered to help. While he was busy with the car, I spoke to one of the ladies and discovered that they were Salvation Army missionaries who had come to town for the weekend from a mission station outside Salisbury. They were on their way to the Bamboo Inn Chinese Restaurant on Manica Road. I introduced myself and explained that we were on our way to a youth meeting at the Assembly of God in Eastlea.

Our new friend managed to get the car going, but as they drove off, we noticed a pool of water where their car had been standing. We followed them to the Bamboo Inn, and our new friend arranged to visit them the next day and see if he could repair their car. We then went to the youth meeting, where sadly, partway through, the newlyweds left the meeting, and I did not see them again.

When I arrived at the Assembly the following Sunday morning, I was somewhat surprised to see the two Salvation Army missionaries standing outside, anxiously awaiting my arrival. I was horrified to discover that the newlyweds arrived to repair the car the day before and took it for a test drive shortly after they arrived and never returned. The ladies had trusted them because they were with me, a believer on my way to a meeting. They took it for granted that the other people with me were all part of our fellowship. Sadly, I explained that I had only known the man for a few minutes, had never met him before, and did not even know his surname!

I had to miss the meeting that morning to find the newlyweds, who, by the way, it turned out were not married at all but were just abusing the trust and hospitality of a friend.

My first port of call was to visit the other young woman as she was not at the meeting that morning.

Sadly, she could not provide much information, other than the young man's parents' address and phone number. When I contacted them, they were not interested in assisting me, so the hunt was on. Where could they have gone? I went all around the City, visiting places that I would never usually visit in a vain effort to find them. After spending several hours in a fruitless search, I realised that I had run out of time and went around to see his parents. The visit may well have been my second; however, they showed no real interest but finally revealed that they might have gone out to Lake McIlwaine. By this time, I had lost my patience and said, "Well, I do not have time to go out to Lake McIlwaine and look for them. We will now be handing this matter over to the Police."

We had not called in the Police previously at the express request of the two missionaries. But things had changed, and time had run out. I had to lead a meeting that evening, and they had to return to the mission station the following day. Having left his parents' home, I made my way to where the two missionaries were staying and told them that I had done all that I could and that now they ought to hand the matter over to the Police.

They agreed, the Police were informed, and I went on my way. Later that evening, after the Gospel meeting, praise God, they phoned my home to say that the car had been returned. The young man's parents had gone out to Lake McIlwaine and found them and the car and persuaded them to return the vehicle before the police discovered them. The missionaries told the police that they would not press charges.

The story was not quite over as the following day,

I had a phone call at work from the police, asking for further details about the stolen car. I advised them that the car had been returned late on Sunday evening, and the ladies have decided not to press charges.

The policeman that I was talking to replied by saying, "I am very sorry to hear that, as the last time we had contact with this guy, he stole a police car. This time I thought we had him, and we could throw the book at him."

I am not sure whether the young lady ever married the young man, but her husband was in jail the next time I came across her. Whether it was the same man, I do not know. However, she appears later on in my story when I was ministering in QueQue.

Another story involving the youth began when I answered the telephone at work one afternoon. It was a call from one of the schoolboys who attended our meeting; he sounded desperate. When I enquired what the problem was, he explained that he felt as if he was standing on the brink of hell and was about to topple over into the flames. There was nothing that I could do for him at that precise moment except pray. I told him that I would see him as soon as I got off work.

A couple of hours later, I was at his home, and he explained what was happening in more detail. He was convinced that he had committed the unforgivable sin and that it was only a matter of time before he would fall into the fires of hell. We spent some hours together, and I encouraged him to recognise that if there was a desire in his heart to get right with God, it was because the Lord desired him to get right! The Lord would not be wasting time on him if he had committed the unforgivable sin. We spent time looking at Bible verses.

"If we confess our sins, He is faithful and just to forgive us our sins and to cleanse us from all unrighteousness." 1 John 1:9

"The Lord is not slack concerning His promise, as some count slackness, but is long-suffering toward us, not willing that any should perish but that all should come to repentance.
2 Peter 3:9

"...whoever calls on the name of the Lord shall be saved." Acts 2:21

Finally, after some hours of having looked at Scripture after Scripture, he prayed and received peace. I laid hands upon him and prayed, and the Holy Spirit powerfully descended upon him. Amazingly, later that same evening, he led his sister's boyfriend to Christ. A glorious victory followed his battle, for which we both praised God. Hallelujah!

All of the things that I have mentioned were part-and-parcel of being involved with the youth. It was good to be involved, and we had many great times, including some amazing youth camps, which took place at least once a year.

YOUTH CAMPS

There can be no doubt that the youth camps had a major impact upon the young people during those years. I have included a number of them below.

A) THE PENHALONGA YOUTH CAMP

I believe this camp took place in 1966 during either the Easter or the 'Rhodes and Founders' long weekend. It was held on the Tatham's property shortly after I was restored to the Lord. I am not too sure how others felt, but I was very conscious of the Lord's presence the whole time. Each morning, I awoke with a song of praise on my lips, knowing that I was restored, forgiven, and accepted by my God. "Praise His name!"

Newby Tatham, the property owner and one of our elders, organised a hike that we all thoroughly enjoyed, as the weather was good and the scenery was stunning. We entered a forest of Eucalyptus trees, and I remember him telling us that the tree pods would only germinate after a fire had gone through the forest. It seemed that although a fire in a forest is generally considered harmful, in the case of the Eucalyptus, a fire would renew the forest by germinating the seed pods.

Brother Tatham tried to teach me a song on the bus as we were on our way home. It was a lovely praise song that he had learned when he was much younger. Praise God for Godly men who stand the test of time and give the younger generation an example. I praise God for Brother Tatham and others like him who served the Lord so faithfully in our Assembly and made such an impression upon my life. Sadly, Youth Camps do not last long, and we were soon back home. For some of us, a real work of grace had been done for which we would be eternally grateful.

B) THE ODZI YOUTH CAMPS

We had two incredible Youth Camps on Cassie Periolie's property just off the main road between Salisbury and Umtali. We possibly would have had more than two Camps at Odzi; however, it was no longer considered safe due to the deteriorating security situation.

To accommodate the campers, Cassie erected two dormitory-type buildings for the young people. I remember taking time off work to travel down to Odzi to help finish off the buildings before the planned camp. My job was to put the window panes in the windows, challenging because I was not skilled at DIY. The first pane seemed to take hours to install; however, I was almost a professional by the time I got to the last pane because of the number of windows and the number of panes in each window.

The caretaker, a gardener and odd job man, who lived on the property with his wife and very disabled son, whose name I have sadly forgotten, was a believer and was doing his best to evangelise the people in the surrounding area. One day, he asked me if I would baptise some of the new converts. I managed to baptise them, with some difficulty, by fully submerging them in a small pool of water. It was by far the smallest baptismal pool that I have ever used.

This lovely man later became the caretaker of our campsite on the shores of Lake McIlwane, where he once again used his spare time to evangelise the area.

At one of the camps at Odzi, our guest speaker was Noel Cromhout from South Africa. He was a real man of God with a real passion for seeing young people saved and going on with the Lord. He and his wife Merle, whom I met sometime later, were a great blessing to me.

On the last night of the camp, we had an enjoyable sing-song following our final meeting. We sang chorus after chorus with great gusto and ended up singing all the old Sunday School songs, along with all the actions! There was a great feeling of joy and a sense of the Lord's presence as we praised and worshipped our God. Different people chose and sang songs. Nadine Hopkins, a nurse, and friend of Cassie's, chose a song, and together, we sang a duet. It was a beautiful end to a great camp.

Sadly, like all camps and conventions, it came to an end. We were soon back home.

C) LAKE MCILWAINE YOUTH CAMPS

Somewhere along the line, 'Youth for Christ' acquired an excellent Camp Site, alongside Lake McIlwane some miles outside Salisbury. I remember going out to the site with three other guys to do a proper survey of the property. One of the chaps was a surveyor, and the rest of us were there to assist. Some dormitory-type buildings and ablution blocks with cold water showers had been erected at the site. There was also a meeting hall which strangely stood upon a huge anthill. The meeting hall had a good roof supported by well-constructed concrete pillars and a cement-coated, hessian wall. The interior was very basic, with railway sleeper benches and very little else. There was a very simple cookhouse next to the meeting hall.

Once we had finished surveying the property, it was time to get something to eat and drink. It was while we were eating that someone suggested that we share our testimonies. Although we had spent the morning together, surveying the site, we had only just met that day and did not know one another. We were happy to oblige. After three of us had told our stories, we all looked at the fourth member of our team to hear what he had to say.

He was visiting from England and we learned that he was planning to become an Anglican vicar on his return home. Sadly, we then discovered that he did not have a testimony to share. He had never asked the Lord Jesus to be his Saviour, yet he was planning to become an Anglican vicar. As we chatted with him, we discovered that he wanted to become a Vicar because he wanted to help people and felt that the church was a means to that end. To be honest, we were all horrified to think of a man entering the ministry without knowing Jesus as his Saviour! Sadly, as we all know, he is not the only person to enter the ministry without knowing Christ as their Saviour! As Ministers, they are 'blind' leaders of the 'blind,' and many of the established Church's problems can be put down to this sad fact!

Some years later, the leaders of 'Youth for Christ' found the cost of maintaining the campsite a drain on their limited resources. I am not sure how it happened, but our Assembly was happy to take it off their hands. Due to the cost of developing the site, we never managed to expand or improve the facilities. However, we did install a 'Rhodesian boiler', which provided the fire was lit, enabled us to have hot showers.

Over the years, we discussed many different ideas to finance the site's development, but they never came to anything. One idea was to develop the campsite much like they had done at Resthaven, the other side of Salisbury. At Resthaven, people could build a house and live in it until they died, but after they died, the house became the Trust's property. Over several years, this had resulted in an increasing number of available properties for people to use for conventions and camps. Sadly, we did precious little to develop the site despite it being such a fantastic property, right on the Lakeshore as things were changing rapidly in Rhodesia. Yet, over the years, despite the lack of facilities, we had some excellent youth camps, and some fantastic Church Conferences, at Lake McIlwaine.

As you can imagine, one of the primary considerations at any camp or convention is how to provide food for all the campers. We were truly blessed over the years to have some eager volunteers for that difficult job. Although all the people who took on this job did an excellent job, one couple stood out in my mind, Bill and Deirdre Wilson.

Bill and Deirdre were always very hospitable and would often accommodate visiting preachers at their home. When I was a married man, my wife Mally and I were invited to a meal one evening. As the meal as being prepared, Bill called me from the kitchen where we were chatting and said that I should come to the table as my meal was ready. I dutifully presented myself at the table to find that my dinner had indeed been served. When I looked at what Bill had presented me, I noticed that it included the potato, carrot, and onion peel, and to add a little green to the dish; he had included the tops of the carrots. I was suitably impressed, but Deirdre appeared with something more to my liking after a few minutes. They both had a wonderful sense of humour ideal for a youth camp.

The Easter Convention held at Lake McIlwaine

reflected the uplifting impact of our youth camps. Bulawayo's youth had not previously made an impression at camps or conventions. That particular year it seemed as if they were all on fire for the Lord. The youth from Salisbury and elsewhere seemed a little 'backslidden.' The Youth Camp at QueQue had made a lasting impression on the Bethshan Youth and the entire Assembly. There is a saying that when the Youth catch fire for God, the whole Church will be revived.

"Praise God enthusiasm is catching."

Before we leave the subject of youth camps, I would like to mention one more. At this stage, I was Youth Leader, but John Stegman, our minister, had asked Les and Avril Helen to act like Mom and Dad to the youth. We were used to having convention-style youth camps and were not keen to do anything different. However, that year, things changed. The youth camp was outside Penhalonga on Newby Tatham's property. Despite our initial resistance, it became one of the most memorable Youth Camps and is still remembered by those who attended that camp with great pleasure.

D) THE SECOND PENHALONGA YOUTH CAMP

In 1971 we travelled by train to Umtali and then bus to Penhalonga and on to the campsite. It had been raining before we arrived, and after dropping us off at the Tatham's property, the bus got stuck in the mud when it was leaving. With the concerted effort of all involved, it was finally able to return to Umtali.

The programme for the weekend was varied with morning devotions and an evening gospel-style meeting. During the remainder of the day, everyone had to choose between various activities.

ARCHAEOLOGY

A group that Newby Tatham led investigating specific ancient sites in the area.

ARACHNIDA and INSECTIDA

A group that John and Yvonne Stegman led to study spiders and insects.

ORNITHOLOGY

A group Maureen Willis led to study birds. As I did not know anything about the other subjects, I signed up for this one. Although, but for a small amount of knowledge gained at Plumtree from my birds' egg collector friends, my only experience was studying a different type of bird!!

PHOTOGRAPHY

It was led by Les and Avril Helen, providing some photographic record of the weekend, which was posted on Facebook in 2019 by their son nearly 50 years later.

The whole weekend proved to be a great success and is still remembered by those who attended. Nevertheless, before we look at the more spiritual side of the weekend, I want to mention a few things.

Sometime before this camp, Mike and Judy Lappan and Ian Webster had come to know the Lord as their Saviour. Shortly after this, at the Saturday evening Breaking of Bread, they were given the *right hand of fellowship* by Bill Mundell, our minister. I remember the night quite clearly as I was sitting with Alan Keeling and Malcolm Fraser, and we looked at each other and wondered what was happening. It was a surprise for us as we had not witnessed this taking place before. All three of us were deacons at the time, and we had never been given the *right hand of fellowship*, and in fact, we had never become members of the Assembly!

You were generally considered a member if you were known to be born again, baptised by immersion in water, were filled with the Holy Spirit, or at least were seeking to be filled with the Holy Spirit, and regularly attended the Breaking of Bread. Galatians 2:9

We soon discovered that Ian was an excellent Piano Accordion player and Mike was equally good on the guitar. As I really liked the Accordion, I asked Ian if he would teach me to play as it had such great potential. However, there was a problem; he only agreed to do so, provided I purchased my own instrument.

As I was never flush with money, I decided to approach my sister, Avril, who had a lovely 120 bass accordion. The next time she came into town from the farm at Inyanga, I asked her to lend me hers for a season and was surprised by her response. She refused outrightly to lend me her instrument and said that I would only learn if I had to buy my own. After meeting with this second obstacle, that could well have been the end of that, but the Lord had other ideas.

Soon after this, I discovered that there was another piano accordion player amongst our young people. A friend had offered him a bigger accordion, but he needed to sell his existing instrument. When I found out that he had an accordion to sell, I agreed to buy it for $50.00 enabling him to buy the accordion that he wanted, for the asking price of $50.00, an excellent deal as far as he was concerned. However, I had nothing to complain about, and all these years later, I praise God for that transaction. Since then, I have had many piano accordions, some I have paid for, some I have been given, and some I have given away. I thank God that each instrument has been a blessing to me and many others.

Ian discovered that I had learned the piano as a child and felt that all I needed was a few tips to get me going and no more, so I think that I had a maximum of three lessons, after which he left me to my own devices. I am not sure that I would have progressed, but believe that the Lord determined that I would learn to play!

During the couple of years before the 1971 'Penhalonga Youth Camp', I had been privileged to attend several camps and conferences in South Africa, where I learned many new songs that I was eager to pass on to our young people. When we were planning the upcoming camp, I suggested that we produce a songbook, including some of the songs I had learned. The book would make the camp even more special, as the Young people would return home with a 'New Song' in their hearts. However, as I did not have the music, I suggested that I teach our musicians the songs by singing them. Once they had heard them a few times, the musicians would pick them up and play them at the camp, which seemed a perfectly good idea to me; however, Ian had another idea and said, "Why don't you play them on the piano accordion, and we will follow you?"

No matter how much I complained, he was adamant (he could be a bit stubborn), so my career as a piano accordionist was born. The music for each of our services was fantastic (no help from me), and I learned to play these new songs. Strangely I do not remember who preached, but they were all very anointed speakers, such powerful meetings that we were puzzled that some of the unsaved youth present were able to resist the

Gospel.

Before the last meeting, a number of us got together to pray, as we felt that it was now or perhaps never, for these young people. God was gracious, but despite a powerfully anointed meeting, they still failed to respond. A week or so later, the Holy Spirit impressed it upon their hearts that they needed to get saved, so they went around to the home of Betty Willis, one of our congregation, who, praise God, was able to lead them to the Lord.

Still, there is one more story about that camp which I must relate. The story began a few weeks before at a Sunday evening Gospel Meeting. The message had been powerful as usual, and John Stegman made his usual appeal. Several people responded that evening, and he asked them to stay in their seats so that a counsellor could come and speak to them. As I was one of the counsellors on duty, I looked around and noticed a young man near me and went over to introduce myself. Having confirmed that he had indeed raised his hand in response to the appeal, I took his name, address and telephone number before I said, "Is this the first time that you have responded to the Gospel?"

He replied, "Oh no, I have done this several times."

I was surprised at his response and the way he said it and then said, "What happened?"

He then replied, "Well, it usually only lasts a few weeks before it wears off."

It must have been the offhanded way in which he said what he said that upset me because I then replied, "Well, my friend, when you are serious about getting right with God, come back, and I will pray for you."

I picked up my Bible and left. I did not even pray for him!

A few days later, I felt a little convicted about how I had treated this teenager, and as I had his phone number, I phoned him and invited him to our youth meeting. Although he lived some miles from the Assembly, he cycled to the meeting and over time became a regular. As our Penhalonga Youth Camp was only a couple of weeks away, we asked him whether he would like to attend. After asking his mother, he put his name down on the list and came to the camp. At that youth camp, he made a genuine decision for Christ and later entered the ministry and is still living for Christ today.

I am convinced those youth camps are one reason many came to Christ and went on to serve Him for the rest of their lives, though they are scattered across the world.

E) THE SOUTH AFRICAN NATIONAL ASSEMBLIES OF GOD CAMP

In the late '60s, particular ministers in the AOG in South Africa arranged a National Youth Camp at Lion's River, not far from Pietermaritzburg in South Africa. As the AOG in Rhodesia was still part of the South African Conference, they invited us to participate. For several years, a small contingent of the young people from the Assembly in Salisbury made the long, almost a thousand-mile trip down to Lion's River. They were beautiful times of blessing, and thinking back, it was a real shame that so few from Salisbury could attend.

Although I refer to one of these camps elsewhere, I want to mention one of these trips here.

On this occasion, just three of us, Malcolm Fraser, Ricky De Lacy and myself, travelled to Lion's River camp. Shortly before this, I had traded in my sound, reliable, and faithful Renault Dauphine for a much bigger Fiat 1800. My old Renault was always so overloaded with passengers that I felt I needed a bigger car. We decided to go in my 'new' car, despite my it having already proved to be somewhat unreliable. I suppose I believed that all the problems had been sorted; however, that was not the case. We made the long journey from Salisbury to Lion's River with no problems, praise God. As usual, the Camp was an inspiration, with powerful ministry and wonderful singing.

Instead of heading back home after the Camp, we headed down to Cape Town for a short holiday. Malcolm arranged accommodation for himself and Ricky. They stayed with Christian friends that he had made at University in Cape Town when he attended the Haarfield Road Assembly. I was blessed to stay with my stepbrother Malcolm Tilliduff and his wife Maureen and their family.

All my life, I have been quite happy to be the butt of a joke, as most people who know me will acknowledge. Even as a minister now for over 48 years, I often tell a joke or funny story where I make fun of myself. The long journey from Lion's River to Cape Town was sweltering, and our friendship was stretched to the limit. My two friends were taking the mickey out of me constantly, and eventually, I had had enough. We were only a few hours from Cape Town when I turned to them and said, "You either stop taking the mickey out of me, or one of two things are going to happen. I will stop the car and lay into both of you, or I will cry!"

Praise God, they stopped so I did not cry or get into a fight that I would have regretted. However, there is a lesson that we can all learn, and that is, "It is far better to encourage, praise, and uplift one another than to constantly make fun of someone."

After Church one evening while in Cape Town, we joined a group of young people who headed off to Kentucky Fried Chicken which I think had recently opened up in the City. It was a new 'finger-licking good' experience for me. We then went up to the base cable station at the base of Table Mountain. The thing that I remember most about that journey was that I had a laughing fit. I do not know how it started, but I could not stop laughing. Even now, many years later, I remember that evening with delight. I have seldom laughed so much in my entire life.

I am not sure whether all the following incidents occurred on that particular visit to Cape Town, but I will include them all here.

The first was a trip to climb Table Mountain, which Malcolm arranged with a long-time friend. When I heard of it, I was keen, as I had climbed Table Mountain many times before and was only too happy to do it again. It was almost midday before he arrived. It is not advisable to climb Table Mountain at noon, in the height of summer; however, that is what we did.

We set out from Kirstenbosch Gardens, travelling up Skeleton Gorge, a relatively easy climb that takes around three hours. It was a scorching day, and as we climbed, we were able to encourage one another by reminding each other that there was a restaurant at the top, near the cable station. We spoke almost non-stop about enjoying an ice-cold 'coke float' (a coke with a scoop of ice cream) or something similar. We nearly ran across the top of the mountain in the direction of the restaurant over the last half hour. We were disappointed to discover that the cable car was not running due to some high winds; therefore, the restaurant was closed.

Praise God, although we missed out on a 'coke float', there was a fountain with ice-cold water where we were able to quench our thirst. Our plan of taking the cable car down the mountain was squashed, so after resting awhile and enjoying the incredible views, we set off down Platterklip Gorge. Despite the heat and the facilities being closed, a climb up Table Mountain is an experience that is hard to beat!

While in Cape Town, I also made contact with the daughter of a friend of my stepfather. I had met her and became fond of her during my backslidden period when she was on holiday from university and staying with her parents in Salisbury. After returning to the Lord, I had written to her about my faith, and she had written back and told me to stop preaching or stop writing. Nevertheless, we met one day at Fishoek, a lovely beach in False Bay some miles from Cape Town.

It was lovely to see her again, and I once again shared my faith with her. I also said that there was no way that our friendship could progress unless she were a Christian. She got up and said quite forcefully, "Well, I will never do that!"

With that, she dived into the sea, and not long afterwards we parted company.

However, a few days later, she called and asked

whether I would like to join her and two friends on a camping trip. They were planning to travel up the West coast towards Saldanha Bay, and I could share a tent with the chap, and the two young women would share the other tent. However, there was one condition, I was not to talk about the Lord at any time on the trip.

With conditions like that, perhaps I ought not to have gone. However, I did. It was a beautiful journey. I saw parts of the country that I would never otherwise have seen. We all got on very well, and the days passed quickly. When they dropped me off at my stepbrother's home, I immediately went to my room and fell on my knees. I thanked the Lord for keeping me and praised His Holy Name. I was so thankful that I was a believer and knew the Lord Jesus as my Saviour!

It was Christmas Day, and I was living with a family of Jehovah's Witnesses. All the same, I decided to get to Church that morning. Sadly, I must have left just a few minutes late. As I arrived at the train station, I saw the train leave the platform. However, before I had time to check the timetable, another train pulled into the station. I boarded the train, thankful that I would be at the service on time.

But I had boarded the wrong train; the train was not going into Cape Town. It was going nowhere near Haarfield Road, where the Assembly was just a short walk from the station. The train was heading away from the Mountain and towards the Cape Flats. It was not long before I realised that the stations we passed were not familiar to me, and I made haste to get off the train.

Having arrived at an unknown station and discovering that the next train would not be coming for a long time, I decided to walk. I had no problem determining which way to travel as I just headed towards the Mountain. It was around an hour or so later that I finally came across the right train line. As it was now far too late for the Christmas Day service, I found myself a seat and waited for the next train to take me home.

I was carrying my Bible, so I decided to open it and read it. I had only just opened my Bible when a man who was seated a few feet from me called out and said, "You do not believe that do you?"

I replied that I certainly did, and from then on, we discussed the Word of God. We boarded the same train when it arrived and continued our conversation. It was evident that he had several problems, and as I was leaving the area in a few days, I arranged to meet him again the next day. When I arrived at his home the following day, I discovered a complicated family situation that I will explain.

He explained that the woman that he was living with was not his wife. She had been married to another man sometime before, and they had had a couple of children. After they had their children, they discovered their marriage was not official, as something had gone wrong with the certification, so they would need to be married again to fulfil the legal requirements.

The woman discovered that she was not recognised as a white person in South Africa and was officially registered as a coloured, or mixed-race person. When the second letter arrived, her husband made a hasty exit leaving her with his two children. It was only then that this second man arrived on the scene, also registered as a white man. He wanted to marry the woman, who was now the mother of one of his children;

however, under South African law at the time, a white man was not allowed to marry a coloured.

This man wanted to know what he should do and was asking my advice? He was considering leaving South Africa and moving up to Rhodesia. I believe he was earnestly trying to do the right thing for this unfortunate woman and their family. I was not a South African, and although I was aware of certain aspects of the Apartheid legislation, having lived in the country for a few years, I was not an expert.

I was also due to leave for Rhodesia the following day. The only thing that I could say to the two of them was, "The first thing that you both need to do is to ask the Lord Jesus into your life. If you ask Him to forgive you of your sins and ask Him to come into your life, He will do so. He will then lead you in the way that you should go."

My heart went out to this family caught up in destructive, ungodly laws. It was soon time to leave. I passed on the information to the Haarfield Road Assembly, but I never heard anything more.

The following day, having appreciated their hospitality, I said goodbye to my stepbrother and his wife, met up with Malcolm and Ricky, and headed for home, a journey of 1,500 miles.

Our journey home proved to be very eventful, as somewhere in the Karoo we heard a terrible noise coming from the engine. It sounded as if the engine was about to fall out. We immediately pulled over but could not see anything untoward, which was not surprising as none of us were mechanically minded. I then started the engine again, and all seemed to be well, but as soon as we were travelling over 30 mph, all hell seemed to break loose, so we kept the speed below 30 mph and considered the very long journey ahead of us.

Around about 5:00 pm, we arrived at a town and headed for the nearest garage. Even though it was about to close, the mechanic was helpful and took the car for a short drive. When he returned, he disconnected the speed cable and sent us on our way. He had fixed the car, but we could not tell how fast we were travelling.

It was great to get back in Salisbury in one piece. We dropped Ricky de Lacy in Greendale and Malcolm in the Avenues but, that was as far as my car would go. It died in Malcolm's driveway. We had travelled over 3,000 miles, and now it died; God was so good to get us home. The car needed an engine overhaul, but at least it got us home. I was later to discover that we did not even have a workable jack in the car but, we were home. Praise God.

'YOUTH FOR CHRIST'

As you have been following my story, you will have noticed that 'Youth for Christ' played a significant role in my salvation, making me sympathetic to their work in Salisbury. For many years, the leader of YFC was Pat Luffman, a wonderful man of God with vision to reach the lost young people of our city. I would now like to mention a few stories where the work we were doing in Salisbury overlapped with YFC.

A) THE COFFEE BAR

In those days, YFC acquired a basement property in Salisbury's centre where they opened a Christian Coffee

Bar. They asked the various church youth groups in the town for volunteers to help run the coffee bar. As we already had significant commitments, we agreed to be involved in a minor way, making ourselves available at various times to talk to the unsaved visitors that they anticipated.

One evening when I was present, I got involved talking to a young man who said something like, "You are not real; you are just a figment of my imagination."

After spending some time with this very confused individual, even I was becoming confused. No, I am just joking. Praise God I knew that I was saved. Hallelujah! Sadly, he just could not understand the simple Gospel.

One evening YFC arranged to show the film called *The Greatest Story Ever Told,* and a number of us went along. While watching that film, I understood the Death, Burial and Resurrection of the Lord Jesus Christ in a new way. That night, the Resurrection of Jesus our Lord became so much more real to me than it had ever been before. Praise God, Jesus is alive! He did miraculously conquer death and rise from the grave. Praise His Holy Name!!!!

Another evening after we had completed our youth meeting, a few of us decided to go to the YFC Coffee Bar, and it was on that night that Barbie Jackson gave her life to the Lord. We must have been talking in my car on our way to the coffee bar because when we arrived, I asked if we could use their little counselling room. I took her through the Scriptures, after which we prayed, and she asked Jesus to be her Saviour. However, I was very concerned for her and that night spent some time praying for her before going to sleep.

Due to my concern, before going home after the

Sunday morning service, I decided to visit her at home to see how she was. When I arrived at her home, she was in the garden, outside washing her dad's car looking radiant with a big smile on her face. After greeting her, I asked her what had happened as I had been very concerned for her when we had dropped her off on Friday night.

She said, "When I arrived home, I went straight to my room and fell on my knees next to my bed and sobbed myself to sleep. However, when I awoke in the morning, I was full of joy and knew that Jesus has come into my life and am sure of my salvation."

Praise God; salvation is real; although her experience was very different from mine, it was equally authentic. Praise God!

Around this time, a few of us decided that after the Breaking of Bread service, on a Saturday evening, we would go into the centre of Salisbury and distribute Gospel tracts and witness to whoever we came across. Just in case you get the idea that I came up with this suggestion, I have to say that I did not, but I agreed to participate. On this particular Saturday evening, I tried to call it off because there was no one available except two teenage girls, Ann and Betty Hutton. However, as both girls were keen to go into town and evangelise, I agreed to take them, provided we kept to the city centre.

After parking the car, we walked down First street until we arrived at Manica Road, with very little success. At this point, conscious that I had two teenage girls in my care, I said we had come as far as we should go. However, they suggested that we walk a little further down Manica Road, as we had not yet met anyone who was at all interested. I reluctantly agreed, and praise God we did have a few interesting conversations after that. All the same, on reaching Kingsway, I was determined that we should make our way back, as we were no longer in the town centre.

Yet, despite all that I said (some leadership!), we eventually arrived at Pioneer Street, at the end of Manica Road, outside a Night Club, near the Queens Hotel. The area had considerably deteriorated since we had stayed there some years before.

It was outside this Night Club that the girls ended up speaking to two young men. They were both visitors from Switzerland but seemed to be quite interested in what the girls were saying. One man said he was a believer and told us about an experience that he had while on his own in his room. As a result of this experience, he claimed to have come to know the Lord as his Saviour. Although he claimed to be a believer, we realised very quickly that he did not even have a basic understanding of the Scriptures. I remember thinking that he could use a trip to the barbers as he had possibly never had a haircut. The other man did not speak much English, and so we were not sure about him. I was not convinced that either of them were saved because we had met them outside a nightclub.

Having spent some time outside this Night Club, I was more and more anxious to get my teenage companions out of the area. Yet, as the two young men still wanted to talk, I did not want to curtail the conversation and suggested that we go to the YFC Coffee Bar, which was not all that far away, to continue our discussion. They agreed, resulting in a good chat with our two new friends in a much better environment. When we finally parted company, they had both been invited to Gospel meeting the following evening, and we looked forward with anticipation to seeing them again.

Despite waiting for our new friends outside the Assembly that Sunday evening, we were all disappointed when they failed to arrive. However, the following Sunday, the one man came alone and continued to attend the Assembly for quite a long time. He secured employment in Salisbury, and we got to know him very well. I was having major car problems, so we were blessed to travel with him (the girls and myself) on many occasions in his Volvo 122S, a car that I much admired.

While with us in Salisbury, he grew in stature as a believer, but sadly, one day, he told us that he was returning to Switzerland. We were all sorry to see him go, but we were all grateful to the Lord for the part that we had played in his walk with the Lord.

Sometime after returning to Switzerland, I received a letter from him, which brought joy to my heart and a little bit of sorrow. I do not doubt our encounter with him was of the Lord, and his experiences at our Assembly had impacted his life for God. It resulted in him joining the Salvation Army and becoming a full-time officer in Switzerland. When I read his news, I was thrilled, and it was a cause to praise God. What a reward for evangelising on the streets of Salisbury!

Anyhow, there was a part of his letter that brought some sorrow to my heart. He wrote, "Dear AB, ... Before I left Salisbury, I felt that the Lord had laid it upon my heart to give you my Volvo 122S. However, I failed to do so and sold it in South Africa. Would you please forgive me for not listening to the voice of the

Lord?"

As you will soon discover in my story, I went through a tough period with significant car problems for some while before entering the ministry. It was at this time that we had met up with our friend from Switzerland. When I read his letter, my first reaction was to write a letter in reply in which I would say, "Dear…, Lovely to hear your news about the Salvation Army. Praise God that you are continuing to serve the Lord. Now about the car, of course, I forgive you, and will be very happy to receive the cash that you got for the car in South Africa! Every blessing AB."

I am just joking but, the thought did cross my mind! Unbeknown to me at the time, the Lord God had my needs in hand, and my brand new, out of the box Mazda 1300, was just around the corner. Sadly, I never heard from him again, but I have often wondered how he got on and trust that he went on to do great exploits in Jesus' name.

B) THE 'YOUTH FOR CHRIST' NATIONAL YOUTH CAMP

On one occasion that I am aware of, the 'Youth for Christ' in Rhodesia received an invitation from the South African YFC to join them at their national youth camp at Komati Poort near Pretoria. They asked if any of our youth wanted to participate. I decided to attend, but I do not remember whether anyone else from our Assembly went along. At this camp, I first met up with Noel Cromhout, who we later invited to be our guest speaker at our Odzi camp. He was a great musician, and I remember overhearing a conversation that he had with another musician. Noel was saying how much Christian music would change during the coming years, and what he said has undoubtedly been confirmed in the years since then!

There were about 500 people at this camp, including a whole coach load of young people from Rhodesia. Several sporting activities were arranged during the camp, as can be expected at a youth camp that size. Among these was a rounders competition between the South African girls and the Rhodesian girls. As the odds were set in the South Africans' favour I suggested to one of the other guys that we try to even up the odds.

When I type the details of this story, I feel like hiding my head in shame, but I will press on. As it was a little difficult to raise a girls' team from our numbers, the two of us managed to borrow a dress each and join the girls' team to play for Rhodesia. I felt that it was rather funny, at the time, and wondered why the South Africans and most likely everybody else was not amused. We were beaten. The two of us had contributed nothing to improve the score!

I am writing this story in Benidorm in Spain, the number one destination for British holidaymakers for many years. We regularly witness stag and hen parties throughout the year. During a stag party, almost without fail, some man will dress up as a woman and wander the town with his mates. They think it is funny, but it isn't, and God is sick and tired of the drunkenness and immorality of the people concerned. Judgement is at hand. I regret my actions at that youth camp, I am a man and not a woman, and I ought not to have dressed as a woman. We need to remember that God has not changed. No matter what is happening in the world around us, there are only two genders, and if you are a man, you need to act like a man, and if you are a woman, then act like one because that is what God created you to be. Deuteronomy 22:5

The trip home was uneventful, but I was delighted to have attended the youth camp and thank God for all that YFC has accomplished over the years. Being involved in youth work was very rewarding, and there were times of incredible blessing, for which I can only praise God!

Chapter 5

ALMOST THERE!

THE GENERAL CONFERENCE IN SOUTH AFRICA.

In 1969, John Stegman first suggested that I attend the bi-annual conference in South Africa, and on this particular occasion, several people from Salisbury attended. The group included John and Yvonne Stegman, Mary Brown, Les and Maureen Willis, Malcolm Fraser and myself, and another chap whose name I have forgotten. I am aware that all of the following incidents did not all occur at the 1969 conference, but I have included them for convenience.

The General Conference was held just outside Witbank, and it included all sections of the Assemblies of God. The black delegates from 'The Back to God Crusade' under Nicholas Bhengu were, by far, the most significant contingent and numbered well over a thousand people. Although this was a large number, there would have been many, many more delegates had all those who wanted to come been able to attend. However, due to several difficulties, including accommodation, each Assembly was only allowed to send a small number of delegates.

Most of the delegates were provided with accommodation in a vast Marquee erected on site. There was a major storm on the last night of the conference. When we arose the following day, it looked as if it had snowed, but it wasn't snow. A couple of inches of hailstones covered the ground. Sadly, the hail stones' incredible weight caused the tent's canvas to give way, and most of the occupants had a rude awakening. Despite this, we discovered that after their tent was destroyed, they went into the meeting hall and spent the rest of the night worshiping the Lord. Their Christian witness greatly challenged us as we were not sure that we would have handled the incident with as much grace.

The next largest contingent at the Conference was from the white congregations who numbered around 200 delegates. Unlike the black churches under Brother Bhengu, it was not a united group as several different groups were all part of the General Conference. The group that we were part of looked to Jim Mullin for leadership. He was a great man of God, and at one time, the Assemblies over which he had oversight stretched from Cape Town right through South Africa, Southern Rhodesia, and up into the Copper Belt in Northern Rhodesia.

His brother Fred Mullin was the Minister of an assembly in the Johannesburg area, which did not look to him for leadership. In time other groups were established, such as 'The Coastal Assemblies' in Natal, who looked to Mike Attlee for leadership, another great man of God. The black Assemblies had one leader named Nicholas Bhengu, who was known to say, "There could only be one bull in the kraal."

He meant that there could not be more than one leader in the 'black work' in Southern Africa while he was around.

Our accommodation was very varied as most of the delegates found lodging at the various hotels in and around the town. However, Malcolm and I ended up sharing a room with several other men in an old, pretty run-down, thatched house on the property. The big storm caused a bit of a problem in our quarters as well. The hail dislodged a lot of accumulated soot from the thatched roof, and when we awoke in the morning, one or two of the chaps were covered in it. The Lord spared Malcolm and me; we escaped the inconvenience of waking up with soot all over us. When we went outside, we were met with an amazing sight, as small hailstones covered the ground as far as the eye could see.

The General Conference's final group were the coloured and Indian delegates who numbered somewhat less than the white contingent. I have no idea where they were all accommodated. One evening while on our way to our sleeping quarters, after enjoying a wonderful singsong with some friends, we heard enthusiastic singing coming from the kitchen area. On investigation, we discovered that the singing was coming from some of the coloured delegates, hard at work preparing the food for the following day. They had potatoes, carrots or other vegetables in their hands, but at the same time they were singing with great enthusiasm,

"I'm going to stay right under the blood; I'm going to stay right under the blood,
I'm going to stay right under the blood, where the devil can't do me no harm!
No harm, no harm, no harm,
No harm, no harm, no harm,
No harm, no harm, no harm, where the devil can't do me no harm!

I'm going to trust in Jesus' name; I'm going to trust in Jesus' name,

I'm going to trust in Jesus' name, where the devil can't do me
no harm!
No harm, no harm, no harm,
No harm, no harm, no harm,
No harm, no harm, no harm, where the devil can't do me no
harm!"

As the words were relatively easy to learn, we ended up joining them and singing with them for some time before we departed and went to bed. I have never forgotten the words of the song and have often sung it over the years.

Not only did these dear people sing with incredible enthusiasm, but the singing during the meetings was such as you will only hear in Africa. One of the songs that they sang at the conference, I have never forgotten. I often play it on the piano. However, another song was even more impressive, but I have forgotten the tune and never understood the words. I believe that it was Zulu, and I was told that it dealt with the Lord Jesus' Crucifixion. As they sang the song, they struck their hands together at the part about the nails being pounded into their Saviour and Lord's hands and feet. It was a powerful song that made the sufferings of the Lord Jesus Christ come alive as it was being sung, even when we did not fully understand the words!

Continuing with the subject of singing, believe it or not, I had the joy of singing a duet with Malcolm Fraser at that conference. It happened when Noel Cromhout, whom I had got to know at one of the youth camps, asked if the Rhodesians could come up with a song item. However, I felt that we, that is, Malcolm and I, could do something ourselves. I had a song in mind. We eventually put a group together, which included

Malcolm Fraser, me, a much-needed musician, a guitarist from Cape Town (far from Rhodesia), and two young women from Pietersburg (just across the border from Rhodesia) who agreed to sing with us. If I had given it a moment's thought, I would have realised that Maureen Willis was an accomplished singer, and we should have asked her.

It was an easy song, but no one knew it but myself, so I wrote out the words and taught it to them. We were to be singing at the afternoon meeting, and as the girls were going into the town after lunch, they asked if they could take the words with them to learn. I should have written out more than one copy, but how did I know what was about to take place?

Just after lunch, the heavens opened, and a big storm delayed the girls' return from town. As a result, when the meeting began, there was no sign of them. It wasn't an immediate problem as there were many song items that day, so we prayed that they would appear in time. Eventually, we heard the leader of the meeting say, "And now we have a quartet from Rhodesia."

As the two of us arose followed by our guitarist, one could clearly see that it was not a quartet, so when I arrived on the platform, I said, "Sorry, it is now a duet."

We had a very shaky start as the guitarist had forgotten the tune, and as we stood on the platform before over 2000 people, he whispered into my ear, "Just start, and I will pick it up from there."

Sadly, Malcolm had forgotten the words, which further complicated things, and the girls had the only copy with them. But, all was not lost, as, by the time we got to the third verse, we were doing quite well. Years later, when I asked Noel Cromhout if he remembered the time we sang at the General Conference, he replied, "AB, there are some things that we choose to forget."

Just in case Malcolm Fraser or indeed Noel Cromhout read my story, I include the words of the song's first verse to assist their memory.

"When first I heard of Pentecost,
I thought it was a shame,
that such an unusual doctrine
should be taught in Jesus' name!
They said 'twas in the Bible, so I didn't want to doubt
and went along to Pentecost to see them sing and shout.

Oh, it's real, it's real, I know I know it's real
it's the Pentecostal blessing, and I know I know it's real."

Please let me assure you; I am not telling this story so that you can follow my example! It is always a great privilege to be asked to sing at a youth meeting, church service, or conference and should not be taken lightly as we need to do it 'as unto the Lord,' however, this is my story. I am not always proud of what I did, and it is no wonder that Noel wanted to forget the whole episode.

Surprisingly, although they never asked me to sing at the General Conference again, that was not the only time that I ended up on the platform. Some years later, John Stegman asked me to lead the early morning prayer meeting, which was easier said than done. Once the around 2000 delegates got going, they all prayed very enthusiastically at the same time! Having started the prayer meeting, when the scheduled time had elapsed, I needed to bring the prayer meeting to a close, as the day's program was full. However, no one took the slightest bit of notice of me; they just kept on praying.

Suddenly, without any help from me, the prayer meeting came to an end!

I later discovered that the man who led the next meeting was a Swazi Prince, a member of the Swazi Royal family. I was amazed at the authority he had, particularly when I considered my own leadership at the morning prayer meeting. However, as I looked at him leading the meeting so effortlessly, I came to the unjust decision that he was a very proud man.

When the meeting ended, I needed to find someone who knew Geoffrey Mkwanazi, who I understood was living in Bulawayo and leading Rhodesia's work under Nicholas Bhengu. As I had no idea who to ask, I decided to approach that morning's worship leader to see if he knew him and where I could find him. When I asked if he knew Geoffrey and where I could find him, he was only too willing to help. My opinion of him changed radically, and I discovered that he was a very humble man who had led the meeting under the anointing of the Holy Spirit. The man I wanted to meet was also very humble, and when we worked together, in the days that were ahead, I came to respect him as a truly great man of God.

It was at this 1969 Conference that Brother Bhengu addressed the gathering and said something like the following, "I am no longer willing to lead this movement! When I hear how some of our ministers are using their cars as private taxis, cars which have been provided to them by the 'Back to God Crusade', to do the work of God, I am not willing to be part of such a movement and must resign!"

He also mentioned some other things, but as we realised that this was not our problem, the white and I am sure the coloured and Indian delegates withdrew so that the most extensive section of the conference could resolve their differences. Others told me Brother Bhengu had used these tactics before. Everybody knew that no one could fill his shoes at that time, but his threat to resign would have caught their attention, and they would resolve specific problems that day.

We withdrew into the dining room, where we then had a meeting led by John Bond. He was the General Chairman of the entire conference, a position he held for many years. I cannot remember the issues discussed that day; however, I remember that the discussion got quite heated at one stage. Whatever the problem was, it looked as if it was getting a little out of hand with strong words going back and forth. It was then that Faans Klopper stood to his feet and said, "Brethren, let us pray!"

He was an elder in the Haarfield Road Assembly in Cape Town, the fellowship that had grown out of the congregation that had such an impact upon my own life. Having called the conference to prayer, he bowed his head and led the entire body in a heartfelt prayer for love, unity, and peace. After that time of prayer, the discussion came to an end, and peace was restored. Ever since that day, I have admired Faans Klopper for what he did. Would to God that more men of that calibre, men who are sold out for God, would be raised from within our congregations!

As we set out to return home, Brother Louis Potgieter arrived with what he called 'padkos' or food for the road to see us on our way. He was a lovely man of God, much loved by the black people in South Africa. Someone told me that he had taken the trouble to learn how to greet each tribal group in their language, which in South Africa was quite a feat. The black population was composed of Zulu, Xhosa, Ndebele, Swazi, Sotho, Shangaan, Tsongo, and Venda peoples, so greeting each group of people in their language was a true demonstration of brotherly love.

At one of the meetings, Brother Potgieter preached a message which I have never forgotten. It dealt with Joseph's story when he was sent by his father Jacob to Shechem to find his brothers. When he arrived, they were not there, and while he was trying to find out where they had gone, Joseph met up with a man who asked him what he was doing. Joseph replied that he was looking for his brothers. The message was entitled, *Ek Soek My Broers!* The English translation is *I am Seeking My Brothers!* His ministry that day encouraged us to seek out our brethren, as we are all part of the family of God and need to respect, love, and care for one another. I have never forgotten this powerful message. In the context of a racially divided Southern Africa, it was a very timely reminder that whether we were black, white, coloured or Indian we were all one in Christ and descendants of one man, Adam. There is much more that I could say about that and other conferences; however, we must move on.

Besides the other delegates, there was a Portuguese delegation from Mozambique, where there had been a major revival. As we were planning to enjoy a couple of days of holiday at the beach in Lourenço Marques, we arranged to attend one of their mid-week services before returning home.

For many years the Portuguese authorities in Mozambique had forbidden any Evangelical or

Pentecostal activity in the country. The only Church allowed to operate was the Roman Catholic Church, however, praise God, this had changed a few years before. A recent Crusade by a South American evangelist led to many Portuguese being saved. The night we visited their midweek service, the building was packed to capacity, with around 400 people present. We could not understand a word, but the presence of God was tangible, and we were so thrilled to be present.

As a result of the growing number of people attending their meetings, the Assembléia de Deus in Lourenço Marques built a huge new building to house the ever-growing congregation. The building also included two flats to accommodate two ministers and their families. Sadly, it had not long been completed when the Portuguese withdrew from Mozambique, and the new Marxist Frelimo Government took control on the 25th June 1975. They confiscated the entire building; however, some years later, they were allowed to purchase the flats from the government, and presumably, they were able to use the Church building again, but I am not sure of that.

After enjoying a fantastic conference, and a great trip to Mozambique, where incidentally, I had my first taste of giant prawns, which were delicious and enjoyed olives for the first time too, we returned home.

THE YOUTH CAMP AT LION'S RIVER IN NATAL

I am aware that I have written about various Youth Camps in a previous section of my book, but I need to draw attention to this one, as it was significant in all that subsequently took place. It was January 1971, and I was now 26. We attended the South African AOG National Youth Camp, which was held annually at Lions River in Natal. As mentioned elsewhere in my story, I had been having car problems and so getting to Lions River that year was going to be a problem. However, God answered our need when one of our group offered to take us in his car. If my memory correctly serves me, there were 5 of us, our driver, whose name escapes me, Shirley Aimer, Judith Willis, one other and myself.

Our driver was a lovely, committed believer who had been a blessing to me as a young Christian when I was doing my National Service in the Army. However, he was also someone who had the tendency to look at you when he was talking, which is usually a great idea, however not while you are driving. He drove at around 70 miles an hour! As a result, on that journey, if never before, I learnt what it means to 'pray without ceasing'. Praise God, the Lord answered my prayers, and we arrived safely at Lion's River, which is not far from Pietermaritzburg.

Before we left on our journey, I arranged overnight accommodation in Petersburg with the AOG minister and his wife. He had previously told me that if I were travelling down South, he and his wife would be happy to provide me with somewhere to stay. However, I do not think he had in mind giving accommodation for a group of five people on their way to a youth camp. Perhaps that is why they went away and left the key with a neighbour when they knew we were coming. To be fair, there may well have been another reason they were away that night, but we were very grateful for their hospitality.

I think there may have been water rationing at the time as they asked us to be particularly careful about using too much water. As a result, when we had a bath, we took care not to use too much water. Apparently, I was very noisy in the bathroom, trying to wash in a few inches of water, because one of the group, Shirley Aimer, commented that I sounded like a hippopotamus when taking my bath. The things that I remember!!!

The Youth Camp drew young people together from all over South Africa, and the organising Committee were all ministers dedicated to reaching the youth of the nation. It was always a great time, and many young people came to know the Lord at these events. As the youngsters who attended came from different backgrounds and many were not 'saved,' there was strict discipline. If someone continually stepped out of line, they were sent home. Members of the committee patrolled the campsite regularly as, by experience, they had discovered that it was a wise thing to do. They were very aware of the great responsibility of looking after other people's children, even if it was only for a few days.

At this particular event, they gave me the privilege of speaking at one of the afternoon meetings. Despite my inexperience at speaking at such events, God was good, and I learned some years later that a young man had a life-changing experience that afternoon. When I met him years later, he worked as a missionary in Soweto (**SO**uth **WE**st **TO**wnship) near Johannesburg, home to a huge population of black South Africans. It was at that meeting that he dedicated his life to God to be a missionary.

At that time, I was becoming increasingly

concerned about my future, and one day while at Lion's River, I went aside into the woods to pray. I had three specific things to bring before the Lord. Although I had mentioned these things in prayer on many occasions, this time was different.

As I have already mentioned, I was now 26 years old. I believed with all my heart that God had called me into the ministry. Hearing a message preached by Billy Winter at the General Conference a few years before, I had determined that I would not try to 'batter the door down' but leave it to God to put me in 'The Ministry. The message that Billy Winter had preached was from the Prophet Amos,

"I was no prophet, neither was I a prophet's son; but I was a herdman, and a gatherer of sycamore fruit; and the Lord took me as I followed the flock, and the Lord said unto me, 'Go, prophesy unto my people Israel.'" Amos 7:14-15 KJV

I had been impressed by what Billy said about waiting until it was God's time. He 'Took' Amos and 'Put' him in the ministry. However, despite this, I was conscious that time was marching on, and if I was going to stay in secular employment, I needed to make use of every gift that God had given me. However, if I was to go into the Ministry, then something needed to happen soon. I prayed earnestly for the Lord to confirm His plans for my life and to do it speedily.

That was prayer number one. My subsequent prayer request was also earnest. As I have mentioned more than once, I was now 26 years old, and as yet, there was no sign of a Mrs. AB Robertson anywhere in sight, so I prayed to God for a wife. I did not want to remain single. God had not shown me that I should do so, so I asked Him to bring a woman into my life to be my wife. It was not the first time I had prayed for a wife, and once again, I reminded the Lord of what He had said at the dawn of Creation,

"It is not good that man should be alone." Genesis 2:18

I agreed with that verse as I believed the Bible to be God's Word. Having brought these two serious issues before the Lord, you may think that the last request was not in the same league; however, it was just as vital for me. My final request involved transport. I needed reliable wheels, the last year or so of my life had been a bit of a nightmare as far as cars were concerned, so I asked the Lord to provide me with a reliable motorcar. Once I had brought these three prayer requests before the Lord, I returned to the rest of the campers trusting the Lord to answer my prayers.

On Sunday night, the last night of the camp, it had become custom to attend the Pietermaritzburg Assembly where Billy Winter was the Minister. I was seated in front of Alex (Bushy) Venter and another young man who were both sold out for Jesus. Alex Venter entered the ministry and, at the tender age of 19, became an assistant to John Stegman at McChlery Avenue in Salisbury. One night, when he was preaching in Salisbury, an elderly gentleman who had listened to many preachers came to know the Lord as his Saviour when this fiery young man preached.

Nevertheless, that evening, they both sang with all their might, which is what we are encouraged to do in Scripture. However, they failed to find the correct note and were off-key as they sang with all their might the praises of their King. I have a strong voice, as many who know me will testify, but that night I was unsure whether I was singing in tune or not, as I could not hear myself sing. Despite this, we had a great service, and the campers knew that what was happening at Camp was all part of the local Church.

It was finally time to return home, but it had been a tremendous blessing to us all once again. Praise God, our journey back was uneventful, and we were soon back into our familiar routines.

A NEW MOTORCAR

My search for a reliable motorcar included visiting several second-hand car dealers looking for a car. However, as my budget was meager, almost zero, nothing caught my fancy, and even if there had been, I was frankly too frightened to make a decision. After my last disastrous purchase, I was very wary of buying any second-hand vehicle.

The Fiat 1800 that I have mentioned had caused me no end of trouble. The day I purchased the car, there was barely enough petrol in the tank to get me home, and I ran out of petrol in our driveway. For around six months, I had nothing but car problems that included an engine overhaul. I finally managed to sell the car back to the garage where I bought it, but then ended up without a vehicle and still paying for my previous car's repair bills. Then, as I have already described, I purchased a little Fiat 600 from my stepfather, which broke down a few days later and needed an engine overhaul, making me very cautious about buying another second-hand car!

Cassie Periolli, who ran a driving school in

Salisbury and knew of my need and some second-hand cars, suggested that I have a look at a couple. However, I do not think that I even went to see them. Then, one Sunday evening, after the service, she told me that some new Mazda 1300cc cars were on sale in Salisbury. She advised me not to delay if I was interested, as they would soon be gone. She was quite correct, as new cars were rare in Rhodesia due to our country's economic sanctions.

My sister, Avril, had married Patrick Dunley-Owen on the 11th of February 1967 in Salisbury. Patrick was a farmer who ran Rodel, a very successful family fruit farm in Juliasdale near Inyanga in the Eastern districts of Rhodesia. For the first and only time in my life, I dressed in a dress-suit with tails and a top hat which I rented from an establishment in the city to attend the wedding. The best man was a cousin of Patrick's and a successful businessman and was very nervous about standing up and addressing the gathering. Patrick's parents never forgot the wedding date as the night before their lovely farmhouse had burnt down. Although Patrick knew about it before the wedding, he kept it from Avril until later. Sadly, although they rebuilt the house, it was not rebuilt to its former glory.

In any case, returning to my story, Patrick and Avril had arrived that same Sunday to spend a couple of days with us while Patrick attended to farm business in town. They were always very welcome as Patrick always brought large boxes of fruit from the farm for my mother. Although my sister had very productive beehives on the farm, I cannot remember if they arrived with a jar or two of honey as well? Nevertheless, boxes of fruit and jars of honey aside, they were always very welcome!

I told Pat of my plan to view these new cars and asked if he would accompany me. He was only too happy to oblige. To be entirely truthful, I just went to look at these vehicles because I had told Cassie that I would go, as there was no way that I could afford to buy a new car, be it the Mazda or any other vehicle.

When we inspected the cars, there was no doubt that they were quality vehicles, fully assembled from Japan. We had motor assembly plants in Rhodesia, but they struggled to get the 'kits' to assemble. Sadly, when the assembled 'kits' were not quite as good as the Mazda made in Japan. We took the car for a short test drive at the salesman's suggestion and were even more impressed. Nevertheless, there was a small problem, the purchase price! After the test drive, the salesman asked me if I wanted to go ahead and purchase the vehicle. My answer was that I would contact him after lunch with my decision as I had to work out how I would pay for the car.

Leaving the showroom, as we walked across the driveway, Patrick asked me the same question, possibly more aware of my financial circumstances than the salesman? I replied that I could get something for my old Fiat 600 and maybe get an HP agreement on the rest. I doubt if there was much conviction in my voice as he then came up with a much better plan.

He offered to lend me the money he had in the Post Office savings to pay for the car. The Post Office gave him an abysmal interest rate, and as long as I was willing to pay back the money, at the same interest that he was getting, he would be happy to lend me the money so that I could purchase the car. To be quite honest, I was shocked at this turn of events. After he assured me that he was not joking, I agreed, and we shook hands on the deal.

He dropped me off at work, and I immediately phoned the dealer and told him that I had arranged the finance and could purchase the car as soon as he could have it ready. When he asked me how I would pay, I was able to say, "I will be paying by cash."

What a story, God had answered my prayer in a most remarkable way. All I can say is, "Hallelujah!"

I bought the car on Monday, a day after Cassie had told me about these vehicles, and on Wednesday afternoon, I picked up my new car and drove straight to the Assembly for the Prayer Meeting, which was at 5:30 pm. However, instead of praising God and perhaps giving a testimony about God's faithfulness, I parked the car and pretended that it was not mine. Although God had indeed blessed me, I felt almost ashamed to have such a lovely car when so many in our congregation were widows struggling to survive on very basic pensions, etc. I ought to have stood to my feet and given God the glory as it was He who had used Cassie and my brother-in-law to answer my prayers.

I am amazed at what God did for me at that time, extraordinarily answering my prayers. He not only provided me with a reliable motor car but also one that was brand new, out of the box. Despite the economic sanctions, not having a 'good trade-in' vehicle, and lastly, not much money, God provided me with a new car. Hallelujah!!

THE CALL OF GOD CONFIRMED

God had answered one of the three special prayers that I had prayed at Lions River and was about to answer the second one. It was late in 1971 when just after lunch, I had a phone call at work. The phone call was from Dave Salmon, one of the elders of the Assembly. The Assembly's oversight used to have a lunchtime meeting every week in Dave's office at the Anglo-American Headquarters in Salisbury. He advised me that they had just had a meeting and wanted me to pray about the possibility of becoming the full-time assistant of John Stegman, our current Minister. After listening to what Dave had to say, I replied saying something like this, "Pray about it. I have been praying about it for around six years. When do I start?"

He told me not to be too hasty as they were looking to ordain me by the laying on of hands at the upcoming Easter weekend. I would then begin my ministry. I put the phone down at the end of that conversation, knowing that God was indeed at work in my life. It was clear that the Lord had answered the second of those three earnest prayers that I had prayed at Lion's River less than a year before.

As I was planning to attend the Assemblies of God National Youth Camp, which took place in January every year in South Africa, I decided to give in my notice at work after returning. That would give me something like six weeks holiday before the Easter Weekend. I planned to visit my sister and her husband on their farm in Inyanga and pay back my car loan and then visit South Africa and hopefully visit various congregations where I knew God was at work.

The Youth Camp came and went very quickly, and once again, it was a real blessing. On this occasion, I did not have to look for transport as we used my car. It may have been at this camp that Paul Lange, who baptised me in Cape Town in January 1965, was the main speaker. He was an incredible preacher. I can still remember to this day many of his messages.

He was a very tall man. Whenever he went into the pulpit (wherever he was preaching), Paul would place his large briefcase on top of the pulpit as it was always a little too short for him, enabling his Bible and notes to be closer to his eyes when he preached. On the last night of the camp, there were always a few 'sketches,' or 'skits,' and on this occasion, Chris Venter, who was much smaller than Paul, impersonated him. It was hilarious! He brought a large briefcase with him and placed it on the pulpit pretending to be Paul; however, I am unsure whether he could see over the briefcase on the pulpit. You have to be able to take a joke if you are going to minister at a youth event.

At the end of the camp, I asked the organisers if we could stay an extra night as we wanted to travel down to Durban for a swim in the sea before returning to landlocked Rhodesia. We enjoyed a lovely day at the beach, enabling us all to swim, but it was soon time to head back to the campsite over seventy miles away. On the way out of Durban, we stopped at a petrol station just outside town to fill up with fuel to be ready for our drive home the following morning.

To our surprise, while filling up with petrol, we met up with a very well-known ex-member of our Assembly who had emigrated from Rhodesia a short while before. (Sadly, his name escapes me.) After exchanging greetings, I told him that I planned to visit Durban on my holiday before going into full-time ministry in Salisbury. I told him that I had heard some good things about what was happening in the Coastal Assemblies and wanted to see myself. The man who was leading this particular group of Assemblies was Mike Attlee. Some years before, he had been an up-and-coming rugby star, and people had expected him to play for the Springboks. However, he was miraculously converted and decided to spend the rest of his life serving the Lord. He immediately gave up rugby and, in time, became a minister of the Gospel.

Our ex-Rhodesian friend was helpful, gave me his address, and invited me to stay with him and his wife and family when I came to Durban. He also promised to take me to see Mike Attlee when I was in Durban. We parted, with me promising to let him know when I was coming, as my plans were far from settled at that time.

I do not know what you think about that, but I was amazed at this incident. Many would call it a 'coincidence', but I felt more inclined to call it a 'God incident'! We could have stopped at any number of petrol stations in Durban or on our way back to Lions River, but we stopped at that particular petrol station and at the same time that our friend pulled in for petrol. This 'chance' meeting provided me with accommodation in Durban and the opportunity to meet with Mike Attlee when I visited a few weeks later. (I had already met Mike. However, he did not know me, and so this introduction would be a great help.)

I SAY GOODBYE TO THE RHODESIA RAILWAYS

Once again, praise God; the journey back home was relatively uneventful. On my arrival home, I immediately gave in my notice, meaning I had one more month as a clerk on the Rhodesia Railways before leaving for good. Although everybody in the office knew where I stood as a Christian, and I had witnessed to most of my workmates during the almost seven years that I had been there, I had not spoken to everyone. I made it my mission to speak to all my workmates before I left the Railways for good. One of those to whom I had not spoken was the senior man in my department, Mr. Pengelly, who I have already mentioned several times.

One lunch hour during that last month, I was alone in my office and about to put my head down for a short nap when I remembered that I still had not spoken to my boss. It must have been the Lord prompting me, as although I knew he would be out of his office at lunchtime, I could not get him out of my mind and eventually made my way to his office and knocked on the door.

To my surprise, he was in and answered my knock on the door, inviting me to enter. I began by asking his forgiveness for interrupting his lunch hour and then told him that I wanted to speak to him about my faith before leaving the Railways. As I began to share my testimony, I told him that the Bible tells us that we are all sinners; however, when I had given my life to the Lord Jesus, he had forgiven me and saved me. I was about to proceed when he interrupted me by saying that I could not be including myself as he knew that I did not drink, swear, smoke, womanise, gamble, etc. He knew that he was guilty of doing most, if not all, of those things.

I am not too sure how far we progressed that day, and as I look back upon that incident, I am sure that I could have done a better job of what I was trying to do. I had to leave it to God. I have no idea how our little chat went down or if it had any effect upon his life at all. Nevertheless, I was able to share something of the Gospel with him that day, for which I am very grateful. He had been very good to me, and I trust that I was a blessing to him.

One month goes very quickly, and the day soon arrived for me to say goodbye to all my workmates and leave the Rhodesia Railways for good. Even though most were not born-again Christians and most never went to Church, I praise God for how I was treated in that department and thank God for the opportunity to work with all those men and a few ladies. I do believe that it was God who put me there, for which I am very grateful.

On the day that I left the Rhodesia Railways, I received my pay-cheque, which included a month's pay, some holiday pay that I was due and the pension contributions I had made during almost seven years of employment. I was able to repay my brother-in-law for the loan he had given me to buy my car, making it possible for me to enter full-time ministry with an almost new car which proved to be an incredible blessing. The six weeks that followed I have often described as being like the Israelites in the wilderness. When the cloud lifted, I travelled, and when it settled down, I stayed put. It proved to be one of the most miraculous holidays that I have ever taken, yet, although it may well have been the first, it would not be the last miraculous holiday; praise God!

MY INCREDIBLE HOLIDAY

A few days after leaving the Railways, I said goodbye to my mother and Uncle Fred and headed out of Salisbury toward Umtali. When I reached Rusape, I followed the signs and took the road to Inyanga in the Eastern districts. I was heading towards 'Rodel,' my brother-in-law's farm, which was near Juliasdale. It was a very productive fruit farm, and I have many lovely memories of visits to the farm.

I had just turned off the Umtali road at Rusape to head up to Inyanga when I spotted a hitchhiker and pulled over and offered him a lift. In those days, my car's steering wheel was often my pulpit, and over the years, I had many opportunities to share the Word of God with hitchhikers. We talked all the way to his destination, which was not far from Juliasdale, and as the farm, he was going to was some way off the road, I took him to the door. I encouraged him to read the Bible for himself and ask God to open His Word to him. I have never forgotten our conversation, and neither did he, as he told me when I met him about seven years later. Sad to say, seven years later, he had still not surrendered his life to the Lord.

I suspect I stayed about a week on the farm before heading for South Africa, where my first destination was Bethlehem in the Orange Free State. I arranged to visit Des and Kathy Nish, who had been part of the Assembly in Salisbury but had left to enter the ministry in South Africa. He was now the Pastor of the Bethlehem

Assembly. I spent an enjoyable few days with them before moving on. They told me that you could go away for a few days in Bethlehem and miss summer, as summer was usually short because the town was so close to the Drakensberg mountains. I had a great time with them, but when the cloud lifted, I went on my way, as my next stop was Durban in Natal.

My friends in Durban made me very welcome, and I soon had a meeting with Mike Attlee. I told him that while I was in Durban, I would like to get involved with the work that he was doing. He asked if I would like to look after an Assembly up the coast at Winkelspruit as he had recently requested their Minister to move to another Assembly on the South Coast. Although this was not what I had in mind, I readily accepted.

Within a few days, I moved in with a couple in Winkelspruit who agreed to put me up while I was in the area, and so my brief Pastorate of the Assembly began. It did not start well, as the congregation was very upset that their previous minister had moved. They did not want me, and one brother made it abundantly clear how he felt. The Lord showed me that all I could do was love him despite his evident dislike for me, which was not personal, as he had only just met me. Not only was I required to love him, but I needed to pray for him and his family.

I believe that God amazingly answered my prayers. Not long afterwards, I led this particular man's father to the Lord, dramatically changing the whole situation. If I had taken advantage of the new goodwill that he showed me, I could have had free accommodation on the South Coast of Natal for years to come. I must add that I never took advantage of their offer.

I was truly blessed to be a part of that work in Natal, even though it was to be for such a short time. While there, I not only had the privilege of accompanying Mike Attlee to several different Assemblies or Bible Study venues, but I was once invited by Mike, not long after I arrived, to attend an interview with a Wesleyan Minister at his home. This dear brother had a wonderful testimony, was saved, baptised in water, and filled with the Holy Spirit. He wanted to discuss with Mike the possibility of joining him in the work that he was doing with the Coastal Assemblies of God. We had a wonderful meeting, and I learned a lot from Mike by being present on that occasion which stood me in good stead in the years that lay ahead.

The meeting ended with the Wesleyan Minister saying that he was planning to resign his position, work out his notice, and hopefully return within a couple of months to take on a church in the area, possibly Winkelspruit.

As already mentioned, I had several meetings with Mike and his dear wife and enjoyed going to various places with him. He suggested that I could go to another Assembly up the coast if I wanted to stay a little longer. I got the impression that because the work was growing so quickly, there would be a permanent position available should I want to stay in the area. Following that conversation, I wrote a letter home to John Stegman and the elders in Salisbury asking permission to stay a little longer in Natal before returning home to take up my position as an assistant at McChlery Avenue Assembly.

I am sure that anyone who ever met Mike Attlee would agree with me when I say that he was a unique man who had a fantastic amount of energy. Not only did he run his own Construction Business, but he also had oversight over several Assemblies and took a Bible Study meeting somewhere in the area every night of the week. One evening when visiting their home and learning of his activities, I suggested that maybe he was doing too much, to which he replied that if he stopped, he would never be able to get going again.

One of those Bible Studies was held on a Friday evening in the Assembly in Winkelspruit, which the fellowship thoroughly enjoyed. I remember that one family travelled around 50 miles from their home to be present every Friday evening. They were accompanied by their two young children, who would be bedded down on the floor during the meeting.

Another one of the Bible Studies that Mike took was held on a Wednesday evening at a large private home. To accommodate the crowds, the homeowner had purchased a lot of chairs for the congregation, filling his large lounge (it could well have been another room) and the patio, which opened up from the lounge. The week before I attended, there had been a baptismal service in their swimming pool where 150 people were present. On the evening I was there, the attendance was around 70 to 80 people who had come to listen to Mike's notable studies on 'The Tabernacle.' Some months later, a new Assembly was established out of this Bible Study.

I only remember attending this meeting once, but was amazed to find that Peter King, one of the Elders from Haarfield Road Assembly in Cape Town, was present. He was in the area for business reasons, and although I did not know Peter well, he and his wife had both come out of the Assembly in Salisbury. The last time I had seen Peter, I was in Cape Town on holiday, and we had spent some time talking together. I was surprised to see him, and he was equally surprised to see me. He asked what I was doing in the area. I explained that I was on holiday before going into full-time ministry in Salisbury, working with Mike Attlee while in the area, and had written home to ask if I could stay a little longer. His reply was like a word from the Lord when he said, "If the brethren in Salisbury want to put you into the Ministry as an assistant to John Stegman, you should not spend too much time in Natal and get yourself home as soon as possible."

I listened to what he had to say, and the very next morning, I received a letter from John Stegman, who also told me that it was time to return home as they needed me there. Having heard from an Elder from a congregation in Cape Town, who just happened to be in Durban, and then the very next day receiving the same message in a letter from Salisbury, I knew that God was telling me to go home. Later that day, I explained to the couple where I was staying that I would be leaving early Monday morning, only a few days later. As Mike Attlee was taking the Bible Study in Winkelspruit the following evening, I waited until I could tell him face to face what the Lord had shown me.

As it turned out, I had planned to leave Winkelspruit that Monday morning. I would not have returned if the Lord had not so clearly told me that it was time to go home. The ministers on the AOG National Youth Camp committee had asked me to represent Rhodesia, and I had agreed to attend a meeting planned for that Monday evening. It was to be held at a hot spring resort some distance from where I was in Natal.

When Mike arrived for the meeting that Friday evening, I asked if I could have a word with him before the Bible Study. I thanked him for the opportunity of working with him and advised him that I would be leaving as the Lord had made it very clear that I was needed back home. I told him that I would leave very early on Monday morning to attend the National Youth Camp Committee Meeting and then continue with my original plans, and finally make my way home.

Having advised him of my intentions, you can understand my surprise at what he proceeded to tell the congregation. First of all, he thanked me for my assistance and then announced that I would be leaving on Monday morning; then, in the very next breath, he announced that a new minister would be arriving on Tuesday. As I have already stated, I was astonished but realised why the Lord had made it so clear that I needed to leave!

The new minister turned out to be the Wesleyan Minister that we had interviewed together. (I just observed, really!) He would be arriving to take up the position as the Winkelspruit Assembly minister the day after I left. When he had tendered his resignation, he told the Wesleyan Church's leadership that he had been filled with the Holy Spirit, and that did not seem to be too much of a problem. Yet, when he mentioned that he had also been baptised by full immersion, they were not happy with him and wanted his immediate resignation, freeing him up to take on Winkelspruit. God's timing could not have been better, the cloud had lifted, and I was once again on my way.

NATIONAL YOUTH CAMP COMMITTEE MEETING

I left early on Monday morning for the Hot Springs Resort, where our meeting was to take place and was one of the first to arrive in the early evening but, within an hour or so, all the others had arrived. They included Noel Cromhout, Chris Venter, Billy Winter, Reg Bendixson, one other, and myself. They were a great group of men, and I was very privileged to be part of what they were doing. While sitting at the table having our evening meal, I started to tell the others about a book that I had read a short while before, because it had touched my heart deeply,

"I would like to tell you about this book that I read recently," I said Seriously.

One of them replied Incredulously, "You, Read A Book?"

"Yes, it was about this woman," I said Seriously.

"About a WOMAN?" (Again incredulously)

Sadly, although I began to tell the story, I probably never finished it as I was laughing so much. Although we had met for an important reason, when this group of ministers got together, they let their hair down and had a lot of laughs. I do not know whether I should mention this, as you may misunderstand, but they told me that they ended up laughing so much that they had not managed to get any business done at a previous meeting. They suddenly realised that the time had gone and had to schedule another meeting, as they had to get back home as they all had churches to run. Praise God that men of God and all great men of God have a good sense of humour. On this occasion, we managed to have a good meeting as well as many good laughs.

The following morning before we all went on our way, we went for a swim as it was, after all, a hot-springs resort. Billy Winter hadn't brought his swimming costume, so he borrowed mine, and I waited until he had finished before I enjoyed a swim. I will never forget what took place next. In the middle of this public pool, at this Hot Springs Resort, a group of men gathered around Reg Bendixson, who proceeded to give a Bible Study while I listened from the side of the pool. I cannot remember what the topic was, but it was beautiful to hear the Word of God being discussed so openly and naturally in the middle of a swimming pool.

Sadly, we were soon on our way to our respective homes. However, it was not quite time for me to return home, so I travelled down to Grahamstown to stay with Noel & Merle Cromhout for a few days. It was a real treat to visit the Assembly, which was mainly made up of Rhodes University students, as Noel and Merle had a wonderful ministry to the student community. They held services in their home, which became a home from home for many of the students. Merle never really knew how many would be staying for Sunday lunch. I felt very much at home in Grahamstown and got to know a lot of the students, and on at least one of my trips (I visited several times), I had the opportunity to minister at one of the meetings.

All too soon, it was time for me to pack my bags, say my goodbyes, and set off home. It was sweltering, and somewhere along the road, travelling at around 70 miles an hour, I must have dropped off, which was not the wisest thing to do. However, the Lord was good to me, or else I would not be writing this story, and I awoke just as I was about to leave the road. Other than that near disaster, I had a trouble-free journey back home, for which I praise God!

THE LAYING ON OF HANDS
SUNDAY 2nd April 1972

The Easter Convention was held at McChlery Avenue from Friday 31st March until Monday 3rd April in 1972, and as usual, we had an excellent turnout. John Stegman, our minister, John Bond and other ministers from around the country were there. At the close of the Sunday morning service, they called me to the front of the Assembly, and all the ministers and elders that were present that day gathered around and laid hands on me, praying for God to use me in the days that lay ahead. The thing I remember most about that day was that I had the full backing of the entire congregation, and in the days that lay ahead I knew that many would be praying for me.

Despite it being such a special occasion for me, I do not remember any specific prayer or prophecy being spoken over me. Still, I remember the incredible love that seemed to be directed at me from every member of that congregation. At the end of the meeting, Antoinette Fourie, one of the young women in the Assembly, handed me a piece of paper on which she had written a particular portion of Scripture. I took the piece of paper, thanked her, and put it in my pocket, but it was only later that evening that I finally got around to reading what she had given me.

The portion that she wanted me to read was,

"The Spirit of the Lord is upon Me, because the Lord has anointed Me to preach good tidings to the poor, He has sent Me to heal the broken hearted, to proclaim liberty to the captives, and the opening of the prison to those who are bound; to proclaim the acceptable year of the Lord...." Isaiah 61:1-2

Prophet Isaiah wrote these words around 700 years before the birth of Christ, and they speak about the coming Messiah of Israel. These exact words were read out by the Lord Jesus to the assembled congregation in the Synagogue in Nazareth a short while after He began His ministry. Having read those words, Jesus handed the scroll back to the attendant, sat down, and said, "Today, this Scripture is fulfilled in your hearing." Luke 4:21

Many of the congregation present that day in Nazareth knew that those words referred to the Messiah of Israel, so the people understood what Jesus was saying when He said they referred to Him. As Jesus continued to speak, they became so angry they took Him to the side of a cliff, intending to push Him over and kill Him. However, the Scriptures had already been written, so no matter what anyone tried to do, He would fulfil them. It was prophesied that Jesus would die on a Roman cross outside Jerusalem and not be pushed off a cliff-top in Nazareth. As a result, He escaped and walked away.

Although these verses refer to Jesus, we are His disciples and are called to reveal Him to this wicked world. The Scripture that Antoinette gave me was relevant as I began a new phase of my life as a minister of the Lord Jesus Christ's Gospel. As I started my life as a full-time minister of the Assemblies of God, my desire was to be used by God in the way that these verses depicted.

Before I go any further, I think it is important to mention that in the white or, English Language Assemblies, as I prefer to call them, I was the first Minister in our movement to enter the work and stay in Rhodesia. All other new entrants to the AOG work from Rhodesia had entered the ministry in South Africa. It is true that some went South and then returned to Rhodesia later, but I had the privilege of going out into the church in my own country.

However, having returned from my fabulous holiday in South Africa to work as an assistant to John Stegman, I was in for a surprise. Instead of getting involved with the work in Salisbury, I was sent off to Gwelo to assist Bill and Fiona Stevenson. They had returned to Rhodesia with their five sons after spending some time in Queenstown in South Africa. They were now ministering in Gwelo and Selukwe and needed some help.

I do trust that my story thus far has been a blessing to you. However, there is so much more to tell, so my account will continue in *Book 2* of Living Under Five Flags. My second book deals with 17 years of ministry all around my incredible homeland! I trust that you will be blessed, challenged, and encouraged as you join me on this wonderful journey!